CYBERSECURITY

T0026635

CYBERSECURITY

DUANE C. WILSON

The MIT Press | Cambridge, Massachusetts | London, England

The MIT Press would like to thank the anonymous peer reviewers who provided comments on drafts of this book. The generous work of academic experts is essential for establishing the authority and quality of our publications. We acknowledge with gratitude the contributions of these otherwise uncredited readers.

This book was set in Chaparral Pro by New Best-set Typesetters Ltd. Printed and bound in the United States of America.

Library of Congress Cataloging-in-Publication Data

Names: Wilson, Duane, author.
Title: Cyber security / Duane Wilson.
Description: Cambridge, Massachusetts : The MIT Press, [2021] | Series: The MIT Press essential knowledge series | Includes bibliographical references and index.
Identifiers: LCCN 2020033978 | ISBN 9780262542548 (paperback)
Subjects: LCSH: Computer security. | Internet—Security measures. | Computer networks—Security measures. | Data protection.
Classification: LCC QA76.9.A25 W554 2021 | DDC 005.8—dc23
LC record available at https://lccn.loc.gov/2020033978

10 9 8 7 6 5 4 3

CONTENTS

SERIES FOREWORD

The MIT Press Essential Knowledge series offers accessible, concise, beautifully produced pocket-size books on topics of current interest. Written by leading thinkers, the books in this series deliver expert overviews of subjects that range from the cultural and the historical to the scientific and the technical.

In today's era of instant information gratification, we have ready access to opinions, rationalizations, and superficial descriptions. Much harder to come by is the foundational knowledge that informs a principled understanding of the world. Essential Knowledge books fill that need. Synthesizing specialized subject matter for nonspecialists and engaging critical topics through fundamentals, each of these compact volumes offers readers a point of access to complex ideas.

CYBERSECURITY ORIGINS

Internet security has become an enormous challenge. Almost everything we see, touch, or use is connected to the internet, including cell phones, wearable devices, home appliances, and even semiautonomous vehicles. The internet is a portal for businesses, governments, and other institutions, providing remote access to trade secrets, medical records, and financial data. And such is the paradox of connectivity: the more connected our computer systems, the more exposed they are to cyberattacks—attempts to steal data, corrupt software, disrupt operations, and even physically damage hardware and networked infrastructures.

The field of cybersecurity exists to meet the challenge of understanding and protecting against such attacks. In this book, I will present the risks associated with internet use, modern methods to defend it, and general principles for safer internet use. These principles, which have been developed over the years by cybersecurity experts, tend to be disseminated to and implemented by businesses, governments, and other organizations for which the stakes are understandably high.

A network, however, is typically only as strong as its weakest link. A cyberattack on an organization often proceeds from a successful attack against just one individual. And if that person has not been trained to identify the key indicators of a cyberattack, they may unwittingly open the back door, or front door, to an intruder. This book aims to arm the reader with the knowledge needed for the front line of the cyberbattle.

The origins of cybersecurity can be traced back to World War II. At that time, cipher machines were used for cryptography—the act of sharing secrets using codes. A cipher machine is a device that is used to keep communications private through encryption—the process of making a message private. These machines were rudimentary but frequently effective methods of secure communication during wartime. During World War II, the primary cipher machine used by Nazi Germany was called Enigma (see figure 1) and the ones used by the Japanese troops were code-named Purple. Both machines had a similar operational protocol:

1. An operator—the sender—at a command post would be given a message to encrypt.

2. The sender would type the message on the machine.

Figure 1 Enigma machine and components.

3. For each key pressed, a lamp would light up. The character corresponding to the lamp that lit up would actually be determined by a pseudorandom substitution cipher (or code). The action of pressing a key also moved one or more rotors inside the machine so that the next key press would trigger a different substitution pattern.

4. On the other end of the message, the receiver would see the lamp corresponding to the encrypted letter.[1]

5. An operator—at the receiving command post—would then press the keys associated with the lit letters and piece together the message (e.g., similar to decoding Morse code).

Cipher machines allowed military personnel to encrypt and decrypt communications. That process is called *confidentiality*, one of six fundamental goals of cybersecurity. (All six are formally introduced in chapter 2.) These days, cybersecurity technologies are much more complex and sophisticated than cipher machines. But it is essential that we understand the basic vulnerabilities of electronic communications.

As computer technologies became more sophisticated and interconnected, they became more susceptible to more pernicious—and malicious—forms of attacks. Malicious software, or *malware*, emerged as the first class of threats to computer and networked systems. Some of the more commonly known types of malware are viruses, worms, ransomware, spyware, adware, Trojans, and bots. (For an overview of malware, see chapter 6.) The earliest-known cases of malware were viruses and worms. A computer virus infects another computer program and spreads whenever that program is used. A computer worm is a stand-alone program that exploits a vulnerability in a computer system, and spreads itself through vulnerabilities or by tricking the user into executing (or running) it.

The Creeper virus (or technically, the Creeper worm) was created in 1971 by Robert (Bob) H. Thomas, a researcher at BBN Technologies in Cambridge, Massachusetts. (BBN designed the first generation of gateways, or routers, for the Advanced Research Projects Agency

Network [ARPANET], the precursor to the modern internet.) Creeper was an experimental self-duplicating program that was designed to demonstrate mobile transmittal of computer applications. It moved between computers connected to the ARPANET (the first version of the internet) and using BBN's TENEX operating system (OS), infected both computers and printers, displaying the message "I'M THE CREEPER: CATCH ME IF YOU CAN."[2]

In 1982, Richard Skrenta, a curious fifteen year old, wrote the code for Elk Cloner, the first computer virus known to be spread "in the wild," meaning outside a closed network or research environment. The virus was installed on floppy diskettes that stored the Apple II OS. When a computer was booted from an infected disk, the virus would copy itself to any uninfected floppy disk it could access—at that time, most computers had dual disk drives, and OS disks were often used to boot up multiple computers. On every fiftieth infected computer, the virus would display the following text (shown here in the groovy style of the 1980s):

Elk Cloner: The program with a personality

It will get on all your disks

It will infiltrate your chips

Yes it's Cloner!

It will stick to you like glue

It will modify ram too

Send in the Cloner![3]

These two cases illustrate how software applications—if they are able to spread uncontrollably—can be irritating and intrusive at best, even if they weren't meant to be harmful. Yet the Morris worm created in 1988 was deliberately written with malicious intent and arguably led to the cybersecurity field as we know it today. Robert Tappan Morris, then a graduate student at Cornell University, launched his worm surreptitiously from a computer based at MIT that was connected to the then-nascent internet. What made the Morris worm malicious was that it created far more copies of itself than Morris intended, which drained the infected computer's resources—this is now known as a denial-of-service attack. Such attacks impact a computer system's *availability*, the second fundamental cybersecurity goal. Estimates at the time claimed that the worm infected more than ten thousand computers and cost the government hundreds of thousands to millions of dollars to decontaminate the stalled computers. Morris was tried and convicted in a federal court.

So why was the internet's design so insecure? Have there been improvements over the years to address some of its inherent vulnerabilities? To answer these questions, we must briefly understand one of its core features— *packet switching*. In 1961, MIT PhD computer science student Leonard Kleinrock published a theoretical paper on packet switching, an alternative method to purely electronic signals for sharing data between connected computer systems. A packet consists of a header and payload; the header tells the network's hardware where and how to deliver the payload, the contents of the message. The concept was later adopted in the early plans for ARPANET by MIT-trained electrical engineer Lawrence (Larry) G. Roberts, who was then working for the Defense Advanced Research Projects Agency.

Kleinrock would later obtain a professorship at the University of California in Los Angeles; his lab was selected as the first node for the nascent ARPANET. As more computers were added to ARPANET, computer scientists focused on software to govern the shuttling of data across the network. An early example is the host-to-host protocol, which outlined the rules by which information is exchanged: the message (or packet) format, delivery time, file type, and other such variables. Today, consumers assume that their internet-connected devices have built-in cybersecurity measures, however that was not a concern for the internet pioneers. Somehow they did not anticipate the diversity and intensity of the cyberattacks that now plague the internet.

The Morris worm attack could have been prevented. Estimates are that it shut down roughly 10 percent of all the computers connected to the internet at the time; that's essentially a cyberpandemic! That worm proliferated largely because the early internet had a flat structure rather than a hierarchical one. Today, the internet is essentially made up of public and private networks separated by *firewalls*—cybersecurity protocols that monitor and control the flow of traffic into and out of private networks (i.e., an organization's local network). A simple firewall would have stopped the Morris worm in its tracks. The internet is now more secure, but it is also more threatened. In the subsequent chapters, I will explore both the threats and modern cyberdefenses. Additionally, I will show how cybersecurity is practically implemented on the internet, and discuss how the field is likely to change with new and forthcoming technologies, such as blockchain technology or quantum cryptography.

FOUNDATIONS

In the early 1960s, people saw the great potential of transmitting and sharing information across different systems, with a focus on the scientific and military fields. The theory of packet switching, which forms the basis of the modern-day internet, emerged after MIT's J. C. R. Licklider proposed the first global network of computers in 1962. Along with early technological innovations came the need to secure sensitive data, software, and applications, giving birth to cybersecurity. Further underscoring the importance of cybersecurity is the explosion of internet (or World Wide Web [WWW]) users, who jumped from one billion in 2005 to more than four billion in 2019.[1] And that's only 53 percent of the world's (still growing) population!

The WWW is responsible for the interaction between humans via technological mediums. The terms *WWW* and *internet* are often used interchangeably, yet WWW refers to the web of information (i.e., websites, files, and other resources) accessible via the internet (i.e., a global connection of computers linked together). Tim Berners-Lee introduced the idea for the WWW in 1989.[2] Since then, a total of four web generations have been introduced. Web 1.0 was essentially an information portal for businesses to broadcast their information. Web 2.0 introduced the concept of a social network in which people were grouped based on common interests. Web 3.0, or the semantic web, featured machine-readable content that aimed to reduce the number of tasks and decisions a human would make, with the goal of making it easier for humans to find information online by training machines to understand the interrelationship between data. This was the advent of what we know today as artificial intelligence and machine learning. Web 4.0, or the symbiotic web, aims to take the interrelationship between humans and machines to an even deeper level. In a symbiotic web, machines are clever enough to read internet content and react to it; for example, the web could bring up the last page you viewed or display ads based on previous searches. With the advent of Web 4.0, it is more important than ever that we understand and implement effective cybersecurity. But to do that, we first need to know what cybersecurity actually is.

The overall aim of cybersecurity is to protect digital assets from being compromised. I mentioned in chapter 1 that there are six goals of cybersecurity. In fact, there are three industry-recognized major goals (1–3), and three others (4–6) that are often neglected.

1. Confidentiality: keeping information secret

2. Integrity: keeping information correct and reliable

3. Availability: ensuring information is available to the right people at the right time

4. Authentication: verifying an identity

5. Authorization: verifying access to resources

6. Nonrepudiation: validating the source of information

Keeping Information Secret

Confidentiality is a principle that is easy to understand because it applies to many non-cyber situations. The government frequently uses it to denote the act of keeping sensitive or classified data from people without the proper clearances; the information is only shared on a "need-to-know" basis. Sometimes confidentiality is used interchangeably with privacy, as in keeping all confidential information in a private or locked container. In the cyber world, people's information is kept confidential through the use of encryption. Described further in the next chapter, encryption is a fundamental part of cryptography that allows for data to be translated into a form that is illegible to those without authorized access. Encryption requires a secret key that is known only to the parties that possess it. Decryption is the opposite of encryption and is known as the process of converting the encrypted data back to its original form. In the digital world, encryption and decryption are accomplished at varying levels of sophistication, but at a high level, they are essentially the same as using a key to lock and unlock our house or car.

There are two forms of encryption: symmetric and asymmetric. Symmetric encryption uses the same key to both encrypt and decrypt data. Asymmetric encryption uses a key that is publicly available to encrypt (public key) and a key that is kept private to decrypt (private key). Symmetric key encryption is much faster than asymmetric key encryption, so it is the preferred choice for encrypting or decrypting data. The asymmetric key can be used to encrypt the symmetric key to protect it from being stolen. The combination of symmetric and asymmetric key encryption is effective for protecting a variety of online transactions. Indeed, it forms the basis for the blockchain and other technologies that have given rise to cryptocurrencies.

The standard technology for keeping an internet connection secure while safeguarding sensitive data being

In the cyber world, people's information is kept confidential through the use of encryption.

sent between the client and web server is the Secure Sockets Layer (SSL). Someone who purchases a domain name is typically given the option of purchasing an SSL certificate, which works like a digital wallet containing information that identifies its owner and the metadata about that owner. An SSL certificate prevents criminals from reading and modifying any information being transferred between websites, including potential personal details. When a website is secured by an SSL certificate, the website address, or URL, will show up as a Hypertext Transfer Protocol Secure (HTTPS), and not just HTTP. A recent update to the SSL is Transport Layer Security (TLS), which allows users to view the details of the certificate, including the issuing authority and corporate name of the website owner.

Both SSL and TLS enable us to talk to other users or computer systems online in a secure manner – through the establishment of a secure communications channel. They are generally used interchangeably, and you will often see them denoted as SSL/TLS in writing. SSL/TLS uses both asymmetric and symmetric key encryption to accomplish the goal of secure data transmission. At a high level, the steps used behind the scenes for SSL/TLS are those depicted in figure 2. In summary, a client (a networked computer) and the server (the host of resources that the client needs to access) contact one another, the SSL/TLS certificate is presented, the client authenticates it, they

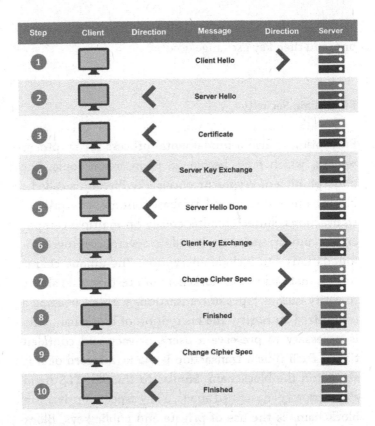

Step	Client	Direction	Message	Direction	Server
1			Client Hello	>	
2		<	Server Hello		
3		<	Certificate		
4		<	Server Key Exchange		
5		<	Server Hello Done		
6			Client Key Exchange	>	
7			Change Cipher Spec	>	
8			Finished	>	
9		<	Change Cipher Spec		
10		<	Finished		

Figure 2 SSL/TLS encrypted session establishment.

exchange a list of supported cipher suites and agree on one, and then key exchange occurs.[3]

Blockchain Security

Encryption is also a fundamental process for cryptocurrencies, which have become a mainstream topic. The underpinning of cryptocurrencies like Bitcoin is called a blockchain—a distributed database containing records, or transactions, stored simultaneously on multiple computers. Cryptocurrencies are based on several cryptographic foundations—to include encryption. The unique characteristic that makes the blockchain interesting is its ability to verify various types of transactions without needing a centralized authority. The encryption of blockchain data is necessary to preserve a user's privacy and confidentiality. Each time a transaction is made, a record of it is stored on the blockchain. Similar to the SSL/TLS handshake protocol described above, a key aspect of privacy in blockchains is the use of private and public keys. Blockchain systems use asymmetric/public key cryptography to secure transactions between users.[4] With their growth in popularity, blockchain systems are one of the primary uses of cryptography today. Given the massive interest, an increasing number of blockchain-based start-up companies have sprung up, and investment in them has grown from roughly $1 million in 2012 to more than $1 billion in 2017. In 2018, the blockchain protocol known as EOSIO generated a massive $4.2 billion of investment in the "initial coin offering" for its EOS cryptocurrency.[5]

Integrity

Integrity is formally defined as "the quality of being honest and having strong moral principles; moral uprightness." In the cyber world, integrity refers to the trustworthiness and reliability of data and systems. A computer user wants to know that the data they create, access, or receive is verifiably reliable and accurate. Integrity is achieved by a principle of cryptography called *hashing*. Hashing, unlike encryption, is a one-way operation that creates a representation of data that can only be verified through the same transaction. When we discuss the primary purposes and use cases of cryptography, they include both data confidentiality and integrity.

Integrity comes in two flavors when applied in a cybersecurity context: system and data integrity. The order is actually important since data resides on a computer system of some sort, so you must be able to trust that system first and foremost. Thus, system integrity is simply being able to trust the system with which you are interacting. This can be accomplished in two primary ways: verifying the identity of the users authorized to access a system, and verifying that the system has not been compromised since the last log-in. The first principle requires the use of some form of biometric data. Most modern machines now have some form of biometric authentication available, such as an iris scan, fingerprint reader, or voice recognition that works in combination with text-based log-in credentials, like a username and password. The second principle is usually accomplished by an OS function called secure boot. Imagine that before you can enter your car or house, there is a scan to determine whether or not it has been broken into. This is akin to what a secure boot does for a computer system. If the scan results in any errors (i.e., something has changed since the last log-in), the system will shut down and refuse to boot until it is analyzed for compromise. The combination of these two principles— biometric authentication and secure boot—provides system integrity.

Data integrity is the successor to system integrity. Why? In the analogy I used above regarding the house, once you have verified that (in general) things have not been tampered with, then you want to verify the contents one by one, especially the most critical ones. In computing, data comes in many different formats, sizes, and access levels (e.g., classified information). Both data and system integrity verification require some form of hashing. As mentioned above, hashing is a cryptographic transformation that produces an irreversible representation of the item that was hashed. In other words, data is transformed using a cryptographic key and function that results in a string of characters that represents that file, application, password, or system contents. This same operation can be performed before the file, application, password, or system contents are accessed. This verifies that the integrity of the item has not changed since its last known "trusted" state. Referring back to the house analogy, let's say you notice that your safe has been tampered with; you may still have an integrity issue regardless of the results of the "house scan" for system integrity.

Three of the top examples of integrity principles being used today are *passwords*, application *verification*, and *tripwire*. Passwords are still the most widely used form of authentication in conjunction with some form of a username. To maintain their integrity and confidentiality, passwords are not stored in their native form. Once you create a password, it will be hashed, *salted*, and then stored. Adding the salt to hashing provides another level of security for password integrity. A salt is essentially a one-time random stream of characters that is changed every time the password is updated. The application automatically updates the salt, without requiring interaction by the user or system owner. The best modern-day example of a salt is the completely automated public Turing test to tell computers and humans apart (captcha). Each time you navigate to a website and attempt to log in, a different captcha code is presented, which serves as part of the authentication process.

In the event that an application may have been tampered with, application verification can be initiated, which is typically done when an application (like a hash) is created and downloaded (e.g., the same hash is computed or verified). If the hash verification process fails, the user should not trust the application.

Lastly, tripwire is an application used primarily for file integrity. By now you can see the pattern for integrity, and tripwire follows suit. Once installed, it will create hashes of all the files you select and update these hashes whenever an authorized user updates the files. On accessing the files that have been integrity protected, tripwire will send an alert if a file has been modified by an unauthorized user.

Availability

In the context of cybersecurity, availability refers to data being accessible when it is required. Availability is particularly important to businesses and other organizations that require "on-demand" access to data. For example, if an online retailer is selling a sweater that is also available on other websites, it must ensure that its sweater is available at the same time or even before its competitors.

Otherwise the retailer is likely to lose sales. Key metrics related to availability are uptime and downtime, which reflect the percentage of time a system could potentially be up or down, respectively, during a given period. Table 1 shows the mapping between percentages and actual time periods. As you can see, even the smallest percentage change results in a lot more downtime across years, months, weeks, and days.[6]

Availability affects many aspects of our online interactions. Many organizations are now using cloud computing (accessing remote data centers for resources, data storage, and computing power) to enable digital transformation (how digital information is used or transformed). According to the latest Gartner report, the cloud technologies services market was projected to grow 17.3 percent ($206 billion) in 2019, up from $175.8 billion in 2018; by 2022, 90 percent of organizations will be using cloud services.[7]

Table 1 Uptime Chart

Availability	Downtime per year	Downtime per month	Downtime per week	Downtime per day
90% ("one nine")	36.50 days	72.0 hours	16.80 hours	2.4 hours
95%	18.25 days	36.0 hours	8.40 hours	1.2 hours
97%	10.96 days	21.6 hours	5.04 hours	43.2 minutes
98%	7.30 days	14.4 hours	3.36 hours	28.8 minutes
99% ("two nines")	3.65 days	7.2 hours	1.68 hours	14.4 minutes

Clouds are particularly important for e-commerce. Studies estimate that 1.92 billion global digital buyers existed in 2019. Today, about 25 percent of the world's population of 7.7 billion people shop online.[8] The ubiquity of the cloud makes the goal of availability all that much more important.

Availability is also critical to governments, and especially their departments of defense. When a business's cyber system fails or is interrupted, business operations and revenue are negatively impacted. When a government-run system goes down, lives can be lost. For example, the US Department of Defense's Advanced Field Artillery Tactical Data System is used by the army and marine corps to provide automated support during conflicts.[9] When a "request-for-fire" command is made to this system, a number of components and subsystems need to be *available* at that precise moment in order to achieve a precision strike. Any interruption to such a system could be catastrophic.

The Overlooked Cybersecurity Goals

There are three goals that are typically left out of primary cybersecurity definitions: *authentication*, *authorization*, and *nonrepudiation*. Although confidentiality, integrity, and availability are the foundations on which the entire field is built, if you cannot verify online identity (authentication), determine what users have access to (authorization), and prevent users from denying that things have occurred (nonrepudiation), you are only solving a portion of the cybersecurity problem.

Authentication

In its simplest form, authentication is usually accomplished by a username and password selected by the user. It is safe to assume that most individuals have had to use some form of authentication online. Its purpose is to verify that a user is who they say they are. Multifactor authentication (MFA) is typically required to access a resource. One of the first steps of access control is the identification and authentication of users. There are three common factors used for authentication:

- Something you know (such as a password)

- Something you have (such as a smart card)

- Something you are (such as a fingerprint or other biometric method)

The combination of these factors provides a strong method of validating an individual and suppling the information required for the next step—*authorization*.

Authorization

Authorization works in conjunction with authentication; it takes place after an individual has been authenticated to a system. Authorization then is responsible for determining the scope of access to a resource that a particular person has once authenticated. What is a resource? A resource can be anything in a computing environment. The most common resources are files (like a word processing document) or applications (like a word processing software or internet browser). All files in any variant of an OS—Microsoft's Windows, Red Hat's Linux, or Apple's iOS—can be assigned permissions. File permissions facilitate the authorization's scope and type. See figure 3 for the Linux OS's permissions structure.

Applications contain similar permissions structures, but let us take a closer look at how permissions work. As you can see, there are four general permissions sections: *file type, file owner permissions, group owner permissions*, and *other user permissions*. The file type section is simple, asking: Are these permissions applicable to a file or directory (which hosts multiple files)? The file owner is the authenticated user. This section denotes whether or not a user can read (r) the file only, or both read and write (w) to the file (i.e., edit the file). The (x) is specifically for applications that can be executed or run. These same permissions apply for people in the same group. For a particular organization, you can have all administrative assistants or engineers in

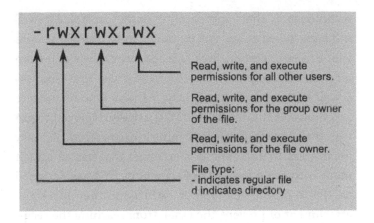

Read, write, and execute permissions for all other users.

Read, write, and execute permissions for the group owner of the file.

Read, write, and execute permissions for the file owner.

File type:
- indicates regular file
d indicates directory

Figure 3 Linux permissions structure.

the same group if desired. The last set of permissions are for "everyone else." For example, this might be people outside your organization not authorized to access the file/application.

I have discussed multiple applications of authentication to include system/device/web access, MFA, and biometrics. The top examples for authorization are access control lists (ACLs) for files, applications, and several network devices. ACLs for files and applications are essentially the same as the permissions I previously described. Network devices such as a firewall or intrusion prevention system (IPS) control access to traffic flowing in or out of a network. They both leverage some form of authorization techniques in their approach to traffic control. Firewall ACLs are called rules. For instance, most companies prevent access to certain sites (e.g., pornography sites) from an internal computer. One or more rules that disallow a web browser from navigating to that type of website accomplishes this block. An IPS is usually deployed to prevent malicious traffic from coming into a network. An easy illustration to understand is an email that has an attachment with some form of malware in it. XYZ has designed an IPS to detect this type of traffic, and then block the attachment or prevent the email from reaching the recipient's in-box.

Nonrepudiation

The last goal of cybersecurity—*nonrepudiation*—is typically handled using a digital signature or something similar. It prevents someone from being able to claim that they did not send a message or authorize some other action, when they actually did. It is most commonly used in email, however it has its origins off-line in the postal service. Postal services offer the mail service of registered mail in many countries. Registered mail provides the sender proof of mailing via a mailing receipt, and on request, electronic verification that the mail service delivered an article or attempted to make a delivery. In this case, nonrepudiation is focused on the recipient—not the sender—but the same principles apply. A second, nontechnical example is a notary public—someone authorized by the government to serve the public as an impartial witness in performing a variety of official fraud-deterrent acts related to the signing of important documents. A notary's duty is to screen the signers of important documents for their true identity, to sign without duress or intimidation, and to be aware of the contents of the document or transaction.

In the digital world, nonrepudiation plays a role in email origin verification, financial transactions, and audit records. For email, since malware is often transmitted through attachments, nonrepudiation gives the sender some form of proof that the origin of the message is legitimate and can be trusted. This is accomplished using a digital signature. If you recall, earlier I discussed asymmetric key cryptography. In this form of cryptography, there is a public and private key. I will explore this in further detail in chapter 3, but here it is helpful to note that the private key is used to produce a digital signature that can be verified by the recipient of an email message. In financial transactions, users are required to provide identifying information before making a purchase and each transaction is associated with a unique ID. This is, in part, to provide nonrepudiation to protect vendors from users making false refund claims for products they have already received. Lastly, financial websites maintain a detailed record of each page visited including information such as internet protocol (IP) addresses. Digital forensics can use this information to prove the authenticity of a user's actions.[10]

Cyber Principles in Action

I end this chapter by looking at a real-world incident that encompasses a number of these cyber principles gone wrong. This attack was so impactful it even has its own website (www.heartbleed.com). Here is the background of the attack, which occurred in 2012 and was publicly disclosed in April 2014, directly from the site:

> The Heartbleed Bug is a serious vulnerability in the popular OpenSSL cryptographic software library. This weakness allows stealing the information protected, under normal conditions, by the SSL/TLS encryption used to secure the Internet. SSL/TLS provides communication security and privacy over the Internet for applications such as web, email, instant messaging (IM) and some virtual private networks (VPNs). The Heartbleed bug allows anyone on the Internet to read the memory of the systems protected by the vulnerable versions of the OpenSSL software. This compromises the secret keys used to identify the service providers and to encrypt the traffic, the names and passwords of the users and the

actual content. This allows attackers to eavesdrop on communications, steal data directly from the services and users and to impersonate services and users.

Remember, there are two types of encryption: one that uses the same key for encryption and decryption (symmetric encryption), and another that uses two different keys (asymmetric encryption). In the Heartbleed attack, almost 70 percent of internet users were affected since OpenSSL was used by about 66 percent of the web servers currently in use at the time. Based on the attack, the private key within the asymmetric key pair was compromised. This was a widespread attack that affected over six hundred million internet sites. A simple programming error caused it, but the result was catastrophic. Attacks of this magnitude affect most (if not all) cybersecurity tenets. The primary result of this attack was the ability for an attacker to eavesdrop. This impacted confidentiality and integrity as an attacker could obtain the traffic of a user and manipulate it before it reached its final destination. Similarly, even if the source was authenticated via a digital signature, since the private key was compromised, the signature could not be trusted as being from the actual key owner. This overcame both the nonrepudiation and authentication tenets. Next, recall that authentication is a prerequisite for authorization. If a user cannot be authenticated, implicitly they cannot be authorized to access a particular resource since they cannot be verified. Due to the Heartbleed attack, a number of websites were taken down to be updated, resulting in widespread downtime across the web. Even though this downtime was temporary, it still affected the availability of a large percentage of websites online. As I have shown through the Heartbleed attack, a single attack can adversely affect any and all of the cybersecurity tenets. As a result, it is important to have a good understanding of how to preserve these tenets.

CRYPTOGRAPHY DEMYSTIFIED

In the last chapter, I introduced all the main tenets within the field of cybersecurity: confidentiality, integrity, availability, authentication, authorization, and nonrepudiation. In this chapter, I further examine the field of cryptography and demonstrate how it enables several of these tenets. To help understand its importance, let's again take a look at the real-world example of Heartbleed, a security bug in the OpenSSL cryptography library, which is a widely used implementation of the TLS protocol.

The Heartbleed bug allows anyone on the internet to read the memory of the systems protected by the vulnerable versions of the OpenSSL software. The flaw allows an attacker to steal sensitive information by compromising the mechanism used for protecting data privacy (or confidentiality). The secret keys are what enable the cybersecurity tenet—confidentiality—which is focused on keeping online conversations private. Even in 2017, almost three years after this nasty bug was first discovered, close to two hundred thousand websites and servers remained vulnerable to it. Thankfully, this issue has now been resolved for most websites and servers. Yet it shows just how dependent we are on cryptography for secure communications online. One "minor" programming error affected billions of internet users across the globe; that's why cryptography is such a foundational concept, and needs to be more broadly understood and appreciated.

Cryptography as an Equation

In its simplest form, cryptography can be described as the study of encrypting and decrypting data—which represents the base functions of the foundational field. The following two equations further explain how cryptography works:

$$ciphertext = plaintext + encryption\ key \qquad (1)$$

and

$$plaintext = ciphertext + decryption\ key \qquad (2)$$

For equation (1), some form of plaintext is translated by an encryption key to produce the ciphertext. For equation (2), some form of ciphertext is translated by a decryption key to produce the original plaintext. In the case of the equations above, the same key is used for both encryption and decryption. This is not always the case, as I will detail further in this chapter. For now, let's break down each equation component. Plaintext is an input for an encryption algorithm, and can be in the form of text, audio, video, and images. Ciphertext is generally described as the output of the encryption process. Or to look at it another way, plaintext is in a human-readable or legible format. To preserve the confidentiality of the plaintext, the ciphertext should *not* be human readable or legible. Here is a simple illustration using a substitution cipher from the Practical Cryptography website.[1] Keys for the simple substitution cipher usually consist of twenty-six letters. An example key is:

plain alphabet: abcdefghijklmnopqrstuvwxyz
cipher alphabet: phqgiumeaylnofdxjkrcvstzwb

The plaintext that I will encrypt is "defend the east wall of the castle" and is shown below:

plaintext: defend the east wall of the castle
ciphertext: giuifg cei iprc tpnn du cei qprcni

To create ciphertext, each character of the plaintext is replaced with the corresponding letter in the cipher alphabet. The cipher alphabet is simply a mapping that denotes how to go from the plaintext to ciphertext. The simplest instance of this is *abc* —> *xyz*. Wherever you see an *a*, replace it with an *x*; when you see a *b*, replace it with a *y*; and when you see a *c*, replace it with a *z*. So "cab" would be translated to "zxy."

In cryptography, a substitution cipher is a method of encrypting by which ciphertext replaces units of plaintext. It is important to note that the simple substitution cipher offers little communication security as it can be easily broken, even by hand, especially as the messages become longer (more than several hundred ciphertext characters). An encryption key is typically a random string of bits generated specifically to scramble and unscramble data. Encryption keys are created with algorithms designed to ensure that each key is unique and unpredictable. The longer the key that is constructed this way, the harder it is to break the encryption code. It is important to keep this premise in mind, as keys are foundational to the field of cryptography and analogous to a physical key. You can have the strongest fortress protected by dragons, moats, guards, and other defense mechanisms, but if the key (or mechanism) used to enter that fortress is compromised or stolen, all those defenses will become null and void.

Confidentiality and Encryption

Confidentiality is one of the key tenets of cybersecurity, and encryption (to produce ciphertext achieves it). As just mentioned, an encryption key is typically a random string of bits generated specifically to scramble and unscramble data. Encryption methods can either be symmetric or asymmetric. Symmetric key encryption uses the same key for encryption and decryption. Asymmetric key encryption uses different keys for encryption and decryption. They both have specific uses as well as pros and cons.

Symmetric encryption involves the use of relatively short keys that both parties can use to encrypt and decrypt. It enables a faster and more efficient use of computer resources by handling a greater volume of data in a given time. This makes symmetric key encryption the preferred method for encrypting large quantities of data, but it also exposes one of its major weaknesses, resulting in the need for asymmetric key encryption. The main purpose of encryption is to preserve confidentiality. To do this, the encryption keys *must* remain private. So if the same key is used for both symmetric key encryption and decryption operations, how can we share it if the encrypted message is sent between parties over the internet and they do not live near each other? One option could be to send it via another medium. If that medium is insecure, however, the key could be compromised and the message could still be lost. This is where asymmetric key encryption becomes so valuable as a supplementary technique—primarily for key management.

Asymmetric key encryption uses a single key for encryption (as noted earlier, called the public key) and a single key for decryption (called the private key, as mentioned before). There is a mathematical relationship between the two keys such that they cannot be derived from each other, and one can be used for encryption and the other for decryption. Although simple, it is outside the scope of this book to describe the math in detail. Suffice it to say, it is a combination of algebra 2, modulo operators, and prime numbers that results in the private-public key pair that enables the "magic" of asymmetric key encryption. Asymmetric key encryption is primarily used to encrypt small quantities of data and is beneficial in situations where you need to share information over an insecure channel. The information can be encrypted with the public key and then decrypted with the private key of the recipient.

To clarify these concepts, let's look at one of the primary cases where both symmetric and asymmetric key encryption are used in practice: public key infrastructure (PKI). According to the Thales corporation, PKI is responsible for most of the security that consumers experience online. A simple analogy would be the organizations that issue driver's licenses. They have the responsibility of creating, managing, distributing, facilitating the use of, storing, and revoking driver's licenses. PKIs provide several useful security properties for the online user. These include (but are not limited to) strengthening online identity, enabling confidentiality, offering security for Internet of Things (IoT) devices, and protecting access to sensitive resources. In PKI, both types of cryptography are used to facilitate a secure connection. Symmetric key encryption is used to encrypt the data being transmitted between the parties, while asymmetric key encryption is used to encrypt the symmetric keys. By doing so, it employs the strengths of each approach: symmetric's speed of encryption/decryption, and asymmetric's secure key exchange.

Integrity and Hashing

Integrity is the second cybersecurity tenet that cryptography makes possible. Where confidentiality is focused on data privacy, integrity revolves around data/system trust. There are three primary cases in which integrity is paramount: using a computer system, sending data, and receiving data. In the case of using a computer system, everything starts with the device or system you are using. If you cannot trust the device you are using, then how can you trust the data on it? Sending data is closely related in that prior to sending data to someone else, you want to be sure you can trust that the data has not been manipulated. Lastly, when receiving data, the recipient needs to *also* be able to trust the system they are using as well as the data on it, including the data received from a sender. At a high level, some form of cryptography can address all three cases.

First, hashing addresses data integrity. Hashing, as mentioned previously, is a method of cryptography that converts any form of data into a unique string of text. Any piece of data can be hashed, no matter its size or type. In traditional hashing, regardless of the data's size, type, or length, the hash that any data produces is always the same length. A hash is designed to act as a one-way function—you can put data into a hashing algorithm and get a unique string, but if you encounter a new hash, you cannot decipher the input data it represents. A unique piece of data will always produce the same hash.[2] So the sender can create and update a hash during the data life cycle to ensure that particular data elements can be trusted. Similarly, on receipt, the recipient can verify the original hash to ensure the data they received is the same data that was sent.

System integrity is a bit more complex, but the output is the same: being able to trust the system. Three main concepts facilitate system integrity: file system integrity, hard disk (HD) integrity, and secure boot. Hashing folders or files ensures their integrity accomplishes file system integrity. Hashing the entire hard drive and everything on it accomplishes HD integrity. Secure boot is a mechanism that prevents the computer from turning off if a cyberattack has been detected. The combination of all these concepts provides holistic system integrity. You can now trust that the computer has not changed since the last time you logged in (secure boot), trust the entire system (HD integrity), and trust the files residing on the HD (file system integrity).

Cryptography and Nonrepudiation

The last cybersecurity tenet I will discuss that cryptography enables is nonrepudiation, a combination of authentication and integrity. Nonrepudiation is obtained through a digital signature or message authentication code (MAC). What is the purpose of a tenet that encompasses two of the other ones? Well, in dictionary and legal terms, a repudiation is a rejection or denial of something as valid or true. Where might this principle be relevant in real life with applicability to online transactions? Again, the concept of registered mail is relevant here. Registered mail is primarily for the sender to ensure three things:

1. An important package/letter was sent (through tracking)

2. An important package/letter was delivered (through tracking)

3. The sender cannot deny that it was received (through a signature)

In some cases, you can even pay for a signature to be required on delivery to enforce number 3 (called signature confirmation). In the digital world, there are several cases in which this is important. Imagine you are the owner of a company and have to fire someone. You talk with the head of the human resources department and their supervisor, and then inform the employee of your decision. The supervisor informs the employee, and they are directed to speak with human resources. To formalize the "transaction," the human resources department sends an email to the employee as confirmation of the firing action along with the terms. The employee, however, did not acknowledge receipt of any termination notice. Thirty days later, the company is hit with a lawsuit from the employee's lawyer, claiming negligence because the paychecks stopped coming without the employee being informed.

A second example is electronic bill transactions. Most companies now have an "environmentally friendly" option, allowing you to receive your bills and pay them electronically. Would this be possible without nonrepudiation? There are several scenarios that could occur without nonrepudiation: the bill payer could deny every month (or whenever convenient) that they received a bill, the company could claim that the bill payer did not make a payment, the bill payer could claim that they made a payment (when they did not), or the company could claim it received partial payment, but not all. The list could go on and on, with either party having a legitimate claim that *cannot* be refuted by the other. Nonrepudiation allows us to easily address these scenarios through digital signatures and/or MACs.

A digital signature is created by using the private key within the asymmetric key pair. Recall that to encrypt and provide confidentiality, we would use the public key to encrypt and the private key to decrypt. Keep in mind that the private key must *always* be kept private. So if we do the opposite and encrypt "something" with the private key, we can decrypt it with the public key, right? Yes. This is because, as I mentioned earlier, there is a mathematical relationship between the two keys allowing one (either-or) to be used for encryption and the other to be used for decryption. A lighter form of a digital signature is called a MAC, which is a block of a few bytes that is used to authenticate a message. The receiver can check this block and be sure that the message hasn't been modified by the third party. This may sound similar to hashing. It is, although with one minor but crucial difference: their purposes. Once a hash is computed, it can only be used to verify the integrity of a message (i.e., that the message was not manipulated in transit). MACs also do this, but they use the private key to create a form of a digital signature that can be verified by the recipient. So MACs are able to provide both integrity and authentication. These concepts are both extremely important when it comes to nonrepudiation in digital communications where denial is *not* an option.

Cryptography Algorithms

Cryptography would be nothing without its underlying algorithms, which enable such critical tasks as data encryption, integrity, authentication, nonrepudiation, and digital signatures. A cryptographic algorithm is a set of mathematical instructions that is used to encrypt or decrypt data. An algorithm is simply a fancy way of describing a set of rules that are used to govern a particular problem-solving operation (e.g., 1 + 1 = 2). Cryptographic algorithms work in the same way, but are a bit more complex.

As stated above, confidentiality can be achieved through either symmetric or asymmetric algorithms. Symmetric algorithms serve as the base algorithm type for transmitting data securely over an online medium (e.g., HTTPS). The evolution of symmetric algorithms

Cryptography would be nothing without its underlying algorithms, which enable . . . critical tasks.

arose based on some inherent weaknesses in the original algorithms that made them susceptible to cryptographic attacks. These weaknesses were primarily overcome by increasing the key sizes used for encryption operations. Asymmetric algorithms are used mainly for online key exchange as well as supplementing symmetric algorithms in establishing VPN connections. When you navigate to a website and type in "'https," and then the website name, a key exchange takes place to enable a secure connection. Also when you send email, some email clients offer the option to digitally sign a message (i.e., verify its authenticity). This is accomplished with an asymmetric algorithm too. Finally, perhaps the most emergent use case of asymmetric algorithms is with cryptocurrencies like Bitcoin or Ethereum. The "magic" behind a cryptocurrency address is asymmetric key cryptography.

The last class of cryptographic algorithms I will describe are used to preserve integrity, and within hashes and MACs. The most popular (yet vulnerable) hashing algorithm is MD5. Previous to it being compromised, it was the algorithm of choice to protect the integrity of files and other digital data. It generally will produce a hashed value of 128 bits. SHA-1 is a widely used cryptographic hash function with a 128-bit hash value, similar to MD5. SHA-1 can also be used to check the integrity of files, but since its inception there have been known successful attacks against it as well as MD5. They have both been succeeded by SHA-2, which produces a 256-bit hash value that is much more secure.

The Other Tenets

I end this chapter with a short discussion of the extent to which cryptography relates to the other cybersecurity tenets: *availability*, *authorization*, and *authentication*. From the Heartbleed example cited earlier in this chapter, we learned that even cybersecurity tenets that do *not* depend on cryptography can be affected by incorrect implementations. To enable availability in the traditional sense, we look to principles like backup servers and other types of redundancies—not cryptography. Yet there are cases (like Heartbleed) where availability could be negatively impacted if cryptography is not implemented correctly.

Authentication uses cryptography in at least two of its forms: the password and public key. The process of password-based authentication is relatively straightforward. A user will register for an account, and then select a username and password. In the back end, the username is stored in plaintext, and a *salt string* is generated and attached to the password for additional security. A salt string is a pseudorandom text string derived from a password. For example, if your password is 123 (I hope this is never the case), a salt string could be "abc." If an attacker is able to discover your weak password (123), they would have to also be able to guess the salt value as well in order to use it.

Public key authentication is an alternative means of identifying yourself to a log-in server instead of typing a password. It is more secure and flexible, but more difficult to set up. The method of authenticating using cryptographic keys is similar to creating a digital signature, as I noted above. The server will store the public keys that the users generate on registration. The user will save the private key on their own machine or device. When needed for authentication, a digital signature is created (with the private key) and presented to the server. On verification, authentication will be granted. Authorization takes place after authentication has occurred. This process uses access control lists that are protected via some form of authentication. As authorization does not use cryptography inherently, it falls outside the scope of this chapter.

CYBERSECURITY IN LAYERS

In the movie *Shrek*, Shrek the ogre tries to explain to his sidekick, Donkey, why ogres are not just the fierce, carnivorous monsters everyone makes them out to be: "You dense, irritating, miniature beast of burden! Ogres are like onions! They have layers," says a frustrated Shrek.

The same is true of cybersecurity. You cannot just view cybersecurity on the surface and expect to understand it completely. But it is also daunting to think about cybersecurity as a whole, without separating it into layers of defense. In this chapter, I will examine the cybersecurity elements and challenges at each layer of defense—people, network, computer (or host), application, data, and the cloud—that underlie mobile and internet-connected devices. Although some cybersecurity professionals don't see it this way, my contention is that the only true cybersecurity threat is people—for example, an organization's employees. The objective of most attacks is to extract information from a host or negatively affect its users. Remove people from the equation, and it becomes difficult to damage a computer system or network from the outside.

To understand cybersecurity according to its layers, cybersecurity experts created the term *defense in depth* (DiD). Just as all cyberattacks follow a similar pattern—called the cyber kill chain model—cybersecurity has a pattern. Let's walk through a realistic example to demonstrate how this works in practice.

First, an attacker identifies an employee who consistently skips their cybersecurity awareness training and sees them as an entry point into a network. The attacker sets up a fake email address and sends that employee an email claiming to be from the information technology (IT) department with an "update." Since the employee missed their phishing and social engineering training, they read the email and click on the link without giving it a second thought. By breaching the first layer (people), the exploit has passed through the network layer and been installed on a host system.

Now that the exploit has been installed on one system within a network, it can replicate itself (like the Morris worm) across multiple systems and begin to target certain applications. Once applications are exploited, data can be stolen regardless of the platform—whether a computer, tablet, or mobile device. So within a few steps, you can see how an attacker can permeate all layers of cyber defense and accomplish their objectives by simply exploiting the weakest layer: a person's trust.

Some experts refer to DiD as the "castle approach" because it uses multiple layers of defense all designed to protect valuable data and critical assets. The approach features intentional redundancies that serve as security fallbacks in case one layer fails. Let's take a more detailed look at all the layers of the DiD model.

People

In cybersecurity, a social engineering attack involves tricking users in performing actions or divulging confidential information. Such attacks have been known to fool elementary school students, office workers, or even the most seasoned IT professionals. According to cybersecurity firm Purple Security, 98 percent of cyberattacks rely on social engineering, 63 percent of successful attacks come from internal sources, errors, or fraud, and new employees are the most susceptible to socially engineered attacks, and 43 percent of IT professionals said they had been targeted by social engineering schemes in 2019.[1]

These statistics demonstrate why any DiD should start with people, not technology. The challenge with defending against people-based attacks is twofold: people will generally choose convenience over security, and people are inherently trusting. With new technology comes new conveniences. With new conveniences come more users. With more users come more vulnerabilities. And with more vulnerabilities come more hacking opportunities. People prefer to pay for convenience, not for security, especially when the benefits of the security protocols are not transparent. As a result, people will always be susceptible to cybersecurity attacks. Technological innovation occurs so fast that it is difficult for security professionals to keep up. Software engineer Max Kanat-Alexander states that

> in general, when technology attempts to solve problems of matter, energy, space, or time, it is successful. When it attempts to solve human problems of the mind, communication, ability, etc. it fails or backfires dangerously. For example, the Internet handled a great problem of space— it allowed us to communicate with anybody in the world, instantly. However, it did not make us better communicators.[2]

The relative ease and ubiquity of internet technology leads to naivete among some users. As Alexander notes, Facebook (and by extension, other communication and social media platforms) makes it easier for people to communicate. But that's not the same as forming or enhancing

People prefer to pay for convenience, not for security, especially when the benefits of the security protocols are not transparent.

real human connection, which depends on trust. In my own work, I've come across and presented statistics that link human trafficking recruiting to social media networks.[3] The reason? People are generally trusting, even of their social media "friends" whom they barely know, and they overly rely on the conveniences of technology. As a result, we face a dilemma that I call the security versus convenience imbalance, which I regard as a critical challenge for professionals in the cybersecurity field: How do we decide how much security is enough without annoying users to the extent that they don't want to use a useful piece of technology? This is a constant struggle. It is an essential one for cybersecurity professionals, however, if they want to successfully provide solutions that the entire world will actually use. As a rule of thumb, we have to assume that users will almost always choose convenience over security. It's why even to this day, if you walk around many corporate office spaces, you will find at least one person's password written on a sticky note or piece of paper.

Two questions need to be asked when designing or proposing a security solution: Is it easy to use? Is it transparent? Even as someone who has spent almost twenty years in cybersecurity, I don't always have the patience for complicated security solutions, so how much less would a more trusting user. Therefore the best cyber solutions need to be transparent (clearly showing the need for the solution) or require little to no user interaction

Figure 4   Google reCAPTCHA.

(thereby reducing the complexity). One great example that achieves both of these objectives is the captcha, which was designed to make it difficult for an automated program to fill out a form online. The captcha does so through a test that requires a human action that cannot be automated by a program. Google's reCAPTCHA simply requires users to click a checkbox after inputting their username and password (see figure 4) to verify that they are human rather than asking users to complete more complex tasks, such as solving math problems, word problems, or time-based authentications, or providing biometric data.

Network Security

The next layer in DiD is network security. The easiest way to think about a network is as a boundary, such as a fence. Your home network is probably the best example of a network you use on a daily basis. Most of us will have some form of an internet connection at home that we use for various purposes: to stream videos, music, and TV, or save data on our cell phone plans. Whenever you connect to your Wi-Fi, you are connecting to your internal home network. Imagine if anyone in your neighborhood could connect to your network. If so, they could not only see the other devices that are connected to your network but also the content you're viewing. How does that make you feel? For me, I would prefer that my internet usage is kept private and would guess that you would as well.

In the physical world, we all have family, friends, and acquaintances in our personal network. When we speak to or spend time with a member of our personal network in private (and not publicly on a social network), we would prefer those interactions to remain private. That's what network security aims to provide.

When the people level fails, the next level an attacker has to penetrate is the network level. Network security can be defined as all of the protection items that are in place to prevent and detect access to an internal set of systems and resources. To understand the technical layers of the DiD model, it is helpful to think about them in terms of the Open Systems Interconnection (OSI) model. The OSI model was created by the International Organization for Standardization, which enables diverse communication systems to communicate using standard protocols that allow different computer systems to communicate with each other. In the context of cybersecurity, the OSI model can also represent layers of defense including the network.

There are a number of devices that provide network security. The top ones are firewalls, intrusion detection systems, IPSs, and security information and event management systems. All network devices are based conceptually on these four. A firewall is a network security device that monitors and regulates incoming and outgoing network traffic according to a defined set of security rules. An intrusion detection system is a software or hardware device that searches network traffic for suspicious activity and known threats, and then registers an alert on detection. An IPS is a combination of a firewall and an intrusion detection system. Once an intrusion is detected, it can automatically be stopped. This is similar to the operation of a firewall when it blocks or allows traffic into a network. Lastly, a security information and event management system is a device that brings information together from all levels: the network, applications, and a computer system. It is most helpful for cyberattacks that proliferate through each level. There will be evidence of the attack at each level that can be seen in a single view within a security information and event management system.

Computer System (Host) Security

Once an attacker has made it through your people and network, they are now at the computer system or host level.

This is usually referred to as the OS, such as Microsoft's Windows, Apple's OS X, and the open-source Linux OS. An OS must deal with potential security issues, whether they arise accidentally or as part of a malicious attack. Modern OSs are designed for multiuser environments and multitasking operations. Consequently an OS must, at a minimum, deal with separation, memory protection, and access control. Separation is the idea of keeping one user's objects separate from other users. An object refers to the user's digital possessions (e.g., files, folders, permissions/rights, application space, or memory segment). Memory protection prevents one application from corrupting another, specifically when they are running simultaneously. Access control is one of the cybersecurity tenets in action—authorization—and focuses on preventing unauthorized access to specific resources.

There are four main types of separation within an OS: *physical*, *temporal*, *sandboxing*, and *cryptographic*. While physical separation provides the highest practical level of security, it is not practical for modern applications. Temporal separation uses the same hardware to execute the tasks, but they are executed one after the other. Sandboxing prevents code from doing something harmful by holding it in a separate container (e.g., a file that has been quarantined). Access to resources outside the sandbox is strictly limited. Cryptographic separation involves the encryption of sections in the memory; it prevents other processors without the key from decrypting the information.

Memory protection prevents one process from affecting the confidentiality, integrity, or availability of another. This is a requirement for secure multiuser systems (more than one logged-in user at a time) and multitasking systems (more than one simultaneously running process). It is accomplished via process isolation, hardware segmentation, and virtual memory. Process isolation is a logical control that attempts to prevent one process from interfering with another. Hardware segmentation takes process isolation one step further by mapping processes to specific memory locations. This provides more security than (logical) process isolation alone. Memory protection ensures that whenever two or more applications are being used at the same time, there is no interference. To illustrate this, imagine you are using Microsoft Word to create a document and are also building a supplemental PowerPoint presentation. If memory protection did not exist, you could be writing in one application, and see that text or image show up in the other application. Worse yet, one application could cause the other one to shut down if memory was handled incorrectly. This is why memory protection is sometimes referred to as memory management.

Access control comes in a variety of forms. The primary ones are mandatory, discretionary, role based, and rule based. Mandatory access controls are imposed by a system administrator and cannot be changed by users. Discretionary access controls are determined by a user. For example, permissions on file access that are set by a user are considered discretionary.

Users can change, update, or modify these permissions at any time. In contrast, a mandatory control for file permissions is not able to be changed by a user. Role-based access control focuses on categorizing access by user type (e.g., general or administrator). Rule-based access control simply defines the conditions of access such as time of day or logistical access constraints. An example of role-based access control would be when a particular computer or file is only accessible during a certain time.

Application/Software Security

Now that I have covered people, networks, and systems (host) security, we should be well protected, right? The answer should be yes, but after people, applications are the main target of an attacker because they are easier to exploit than an OS. There are a few reasons for this, but one of the main ones is that applications are designed to require more frequent updates than an OS. The components of an OS are pretty standard—some of which I discussed in the previous section. They rarely need to be replaced or updated. Yet applications have many more features than a standard OS. For instance, Microsoft Word has well over a hundred features as well as the option to include others through add-ons such as macros. In computing, a macro is defined as a single instruction that expands automatically into a set of instructions in order to perform a particular task. An example of a macro is setting the font to Arial or Times New Roman each time you open Microsoft Office or PowerPoint. Think about the implications of this. One major implication goes back to the attack vector (or layer) of people. Once we get accustomed to using a particular application, we use it without thinking about security. When was the last time you thought about security before opening a Word file? Even as I composed this manuscript in Word, I certainly didn't. This is a prime case of the convenience versus security dilemma.

There are a number of application-based security tools that are designed to protect against application-based attacks, such as antivirus or antimalware software. This is what application security tools mostly rely on: knowing how an attack looks beforehand. This is called a signature of an attack—the attack's characteristics. Once this signature is known, a rule could be designed to look for these characteristics and stop them before they cause damage. But there is a class of attacks called zero-day attacks, which most commonly target a vulnerability that has not been addressed or found. Since these types of attacks are not known, it is impossible to create a signature (rule) to look for the characteristics.

There are many techniques that have been proposed in research to prevent zero-day attacks from occurring. A simple search on Google Scholar for "zero-day attack prevention" yields close to two hundred thousand results, both citations (papers) and patent ideas. In my opinion, however, the design of more secure software should really be the focus of application security. This is the most proactive form of prevention. For example, in the typical life cycle of software, the goal is to produce software with the highest quality and lowest cost in the shortest time. The main steps include planning, designing, building, testing, and deployment. See anything missing? Yes! Security. So if this broadly accepted and taught framework for software development does not have security in any of its stages, how can secure software be the result of any development effort?

As indicated, it is common practice to perform security-related activities only as part of testing. This after-the-fact technique usually results in a high number of issues discovered too late (or not discovered at all). It is a far better practice to integrate activities across the software development process to help discover and reduce vulnerabilities early on, effectively building security in. The concept of a secure software development integrates such security measures as penetration testing, code review, and architecture analysis into the process. Let's go back to our example of a macro. Since on the surface it appears to perform one function but can decompose into others, how could we plan for this during software development? During the planning and design phases, we could lay out all the instructions ahead of time. Let's call them instructions one, two, and three for simplicity, where one = open file, two = write some text to file, and three = save/close file. During the building phase (i.e., actually writing the application code), we only write those three instructions. In the predeployment testing phase, we test to make sure the program is not executing additional instructions (e.g., opening additional files), and once the application is deployed, we can verify the execution of *only* those three instructions. This makes our application predictable. Therefore if it goes outside the bounds of what is expected, it can be stopped. Even though this is a simple case, it is a powerful concept in application security. The more these principles are taught in conjunction with other application development concepts, the more secure code will be.

Data Security

In most cyberattacks, the most valuable asset to an attacker is data—for instance, a password or some other form of personal identifier like a social security number. Data typically resides in multiple states: at rest (not in use), in transit (being sent from one location to another), and in process (being used). For the purposes of confidentiality, integrity, and availability (primarily), data has to be protected in each of these states, and the protection mechanisms vary by state. Data-at-rest protection is the simplest of the three because it is accomplished by either encryption, access control, or a mix of both. I have discussed both mechanisms already.

If, for example, data is created and encrypted, and the encryption key is password protected, there would be fewer data breaches. One of the main challenges with protecting data at rest is key management. Asymmetric key encryption can help with this, yet it is still a challenge to consider when it comes to data-at-rest protection. Even so, the real challenges come into play because data has to be used. Data-in-transit protection adds a level of complexity to the data security issue, but is mainly handled via asymmetric key encryption. In short, if you want to send data from one person (or place) to another, you would encrypt the data with the recipient's public key, and then they can decrypt it on the other end with their private key. I will explore this further in chapter 7 when I introduce VPNs.

Last but not least, there are some cases where we need to protect data while it is in use. For that to work with encrypted data, we need a scheme that allows computations to be performed on the data that don't decrypt it. A homomorphic encryption scheme allows for true end-to-end encryption, meaning the data can remain encrypted at rest, in use, and in transit. A number of practical applications for homomorphic encryption exist. I challenge you to think of other use cases, but here are two to consider.

Encrypted search: There are times when it would be beneficial to hide your search query from the all-knowing search engines developed by Google, Microsoft (Bing), Yahoo, and others. Say you are trying to investigate some research topics or conduct a market survey to examine a potential business idea you are trying to pursue. It would be helpful if this was kept private until the research results were published or after the business launch date.

Electronic voting: Also known as e-voting, voting in this manner uses electronic means to either aid or administer the casting and counting votes.[4] By their very nature, votes must be kept private. The option to vote electronically is a great convenience, however there are many opportunities to manipulate votes that are cast this way. Homomorphic encryption can provide a means to facilitate e-voting in a secure manner. All aspects—voting, tallying, and the results—could be kept private.

Cloud and Mobile Security

I end this chapter with a short look at the security behind cloud and mobile platforms. They each have their own unique challenges for various reasons. First, cloud security is shared between the provider and cloud customer based on the service model selected. Figure 5 depicts the primary service models in the cloud: infrastructure, platform, and application. These service models indicate the security responsibilities of the customer and cloud provider. In an infrastructure-as-a-service model, the customer is responsible for the security of the data, application, runtime, middleware, and OS, while the cloud provider is responsible for the security of the virtual machines, servers, storage, and networking components. As shown in figure 5, the customer's security responsibility decreases based on the service model, while the cloud provider's security responsibility increases. This is due to the fact that the customer has less control in both platform-as-a-service and software-as-a-service models.

Regarding mobile devices, the most common ones on the market are based on Android, Linux, or iOS. The architecture of an Android device consists of the application space, application framework, various libraries, runtime environment, and a Linux kernel. An iOS device is slightly simpler, and consists of application space, core services, security services, and the core OS. At a high level,

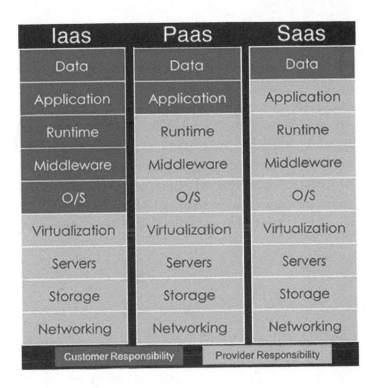

Figure 5 Cloud service models.

attackers will target the components of these architectures, focusing on gaining access to data storage, binaries (executables or applications), and the platform itself. Thus mobile device/application security measures should concentrate on securing these components. Mobile app security requirements aren't much different from a traditional system's. Mobile app security is not integral to the software development process, app developers are not familiar with the underlying system infrastructure, and users prefer convenience over security—which all adds up to a number of threats that can be exploited by an adversary.

WHO ATTACKED ME?

Growing up, we used to play a game where you would tap someone on one side of their body and duck or hide before they saw who it was. Through your own laughter, you could often hear them asking, "Who hit me?" and see them looking around, confused.

Determining "who did it" is called attribution, and it's an important challenge in the field of cybersecurity. Attribution in cybersecurity is the process of a digital forensics investigation to determine the who, why, what, where, and how of a cyberattack. A single attack can comprise many variables, including multiple steps (e.g., social engineering and then data theft), polymorphic code (i.e., code that changes), various attack methods (e.g., social engineering, denial-of-service attacks, or deception-based methods), or multiple participants (i.e., collaborative attacks). So like the childhood game I described, it could be difficult to determine who attacked you.

To simplify the challenge, cybersecurity is segmented into three main categories: *threats*, *vulnerabilities*, and *risks*. A threat is a potential digital event that could cause damage to an information system or network. For example, for an e-commerce website, a potential threat could be that the website could be taken down for a period of time, resulting in a loss of revenue since products cannot be sold. A vulnerability is a potential threat due to some form of weakness or error in a system. Computer programming errors, for instance, typically result in some form of a vulnerability. Using the same example of the e-commerce website, let's assume that there is a programming error that allows someone to purchase a particular item for less than the advertised price. This would be considered a vulnerability. The threat in this case would be that someone could purchase a product for less than the advertised cost because of the error.

Lastly, a risk takes into account threats, vulnerabilities, and consequences. It is a measure of the likelihood of a cyberattack given certain conditions. This likelihood is a rough measure that describes the chances that a given vulnerability will be discovered and used by an attacker (or a "threat actor" in cybersecurity parlance). Using our e-commerce website illustration, cybersecurity professionals would not only consider the threat of the erroneous product purchase but also the likelihood that a programmer would actually make that error. In that case, the risk would be low since coding for e-commerce transactions is common, and it's unlikely that a programmer would make that error.

Cyber Threats

When designing a cybersecurity system, tool (application), or methodology, cyber threats (or possible attacks) are the first thing to which cybersecurity professionals pay attention. Security experts need to be as imaginative as they can in order to come up with a wide variety of possible attacks. By anticipating attacks, cybersecurity professionals can guard against them. There are many types of cyber threats that have been identified over the years. Oftentimes, people outside of cybersecurity confuse threats with types of attacks. For example, if you Google cyber threats, attacks such as ransomware will come up. Ransomware is an attack that encrypts (locks) either your entire hard drive, critical files, or even web resources (web server), and forces you to pay a fine to decrypt (unlock) that particular resource. This is *not* the threat. This is the attack. The threat would be the availability of your hard drive, critical files, or a web resource that could be compromised. This threat might not be realized until after the fact, through an attack such as ransomware or some other type of denial-of-service attack. This distinction between an attack and a threat is important to understand, and will assist you to better recognize vulnerabilities and risks as well.

For the purposes of this book, I will define a cyber threat as an event that could impact one or more of the cybersecurity tenets I previously introduced, summarized in table 2.

Now that we have a working definition and understanding of what a cyber threat is, let's consider the common sources of these threats. One of the more succinct

Table 2 Cyber Threats

Cyber tenet	Definition	Cyber threat
Confidentiality	Keeping information secret	Information will not be kept secret
Integrity	Keeping information correct and reliable	Information cannot be trusted
Availability	Ensuring information is available to the right people at the right time	Information will not be available when it is needed
Authentication	Verifying an identity	Identity cannot be verified
Authorization	Verifying access to resources	Access to resources cannot be verified
Nonrepudiation	Validating the source of the information	The source of the information received cannot be verified

lists of cyber threat sources comes from a 2017 Secure-Works article.[1] It shows the following sources (or actors): nation-states or national governments, terrorists, industrial spies, organized crime groups, script kiddies, hacktivists and hackers, business competitors, and disgruntled insiders. As you can see, there are a range of threat sources and associated motivations. I will not be deconstructing these sources further since they are not necessarily foundational to the field. Nevertheless, it is important to appreciate how serious cyber threats can be given the amount of resources being put behind some of the aforementioned groups of offenders (e.g., national governments).

In the remainder of this chapter, I will explore threats, vulnerabilities, and risks in the context of some commonly attacked targets: web applications. The Open Web Application Security Project (OWASP) is an international nonprofit organization of security experts dedicated to web application security. It represents the highest security risks to web applications, according to these experts. The latest top ten web application security risks are broken down in table 3.

Cyber Vulnerabilities

Once threats have been enumerated and identified, cybersecurity experts use the concept of vulnerabilities to

Table 3 OWASP Top Ten Risks

Risk	Sample attack result
Injection	Attackers can issue requests to the web application that will result in a return of sensitive data on the website (e.g., passwords).
Broken authentication	Attackers can supply the incorrect username and password, and be granted access to the web application.
Sensitive data exposure	User supplies the username and password to the web application, and the information is seen by an adversary because it is not encrypted.
XML external entities	Attackers are allowed to upload XML directly to the web application, causing a potential disclosure of sensitive information.
Broken access control	Attackers can access web application functions directly without proper authentication. This could result in the theft of sensitive information.
Security misconfiguration	Attackers will be able to exploit a feature of the web application that was not set up correctly. For example, if the authentication for the application is not set up correctly, it could allow access to unauthorized users.
Cross-site scripting	Attacker inserts a malicious application into a web application that will execute in another user's browser. This can result in that user's credentials being sent to the attacker.
Insecure deserialization	Object serialization is the process of saving the state of an object so it can be sent from source to destination (or saved and restored) while maintaining that state. If the deserialization of an object on a web application is not handled securely, data leakage can occur. *Note*: This is a highly difficult attack to execute.

Table 3 (continued)

Risk	Sample attack result
Using unknown components with known vulnerabilities	Web application owners are (intentionally or unintentionally) using vulnerable components that can be exploited by an attacker.
Insufficient logging and monitoring	Attacks are not discovered because web application owners are not collecting information about who is interacting with their application.

determine what can actually be exploited. A vulnerability is a cybersecurity term that refers to a flaw in a system that can leave it open to attack. There are many types of vulnerabilities that can impact a network or information system, such as software bugs, weak passwords, web application security flaws, or buffer overflows. It is important to think of vulnerabilities in a broader sense too, similar to cyber threats. Let's reexamine table 2 with these vulnerabilities in mind. In table 4, I enumerate the type(s) of vulnerabilities that could be leveraged to exploit the associated threat in a web application based on the OWASP top ten.

Once you have an understanding of vulnerability types, you can look for specific vulnerabilities applicable to your web application. To help you do this, you can reference the Common Vulnerabilities and Exposures (CVE) list. The CVE represents all publicly known cybersecurity vulnerabilities, which is an important asset for the creation of cybersecurity products and services. It is a list

Table 4 Cyber Vulnerabilities

Cyber tenet	Cyber threat	Cyber vulnerability example
Confidentiality	Information will not be kept secret	Attackers can expose data at rest, in transit, or in process using an injection or cross-site scripting attack to expose database records
Integrity	Information cannot be trusted	Attackers can manipulate data at rest, in transit, or in process using the fact that insufficient logging is done at the server
Availability	Information will not be available when it is needed	Attackers can block access to a web application by exploiting a publicly known security misconfiguration
Authentication	Identity cannot be verified	Attackers can masquerade as another user by exploiting a broken access control vulnerability in the web application
Authorization	Access to resources cannot be verified	Attackers can gain unauthorized access to resources (ones they do *not* own) by exploiting a sensitive data exposure vulnerability in the web application
Nonrepudiation	The source of information received cannot be verified	Attackers can send a malicious message and deny they sent it based on using a web application component with a known vulnerability

of entries—each containing an identification number, description, and at least one public reference—for publicly known cybersecurity vulnerabilities. CVE entries are used to create numerous cybersecurity products and services around the world, including the US National Vulnerability Database. The CVE Details website takes the information from the CVE site and categorizes vulnerabilities based on the type of attack they enable. Let us assume you are running a Linux server, manufactured by Red Hat. Looking at the CVE Details site for a Red Hat Linux server, we see that most of the vulnerabilities in 2019 were related to code execution. This means that *each* vulnerability in that category represents a threat that could potentially be exploited. These vulnerabilities are not a concern for a nonnefarious application code that is running on the server. An attacker, though, could easily use these publicly available vulnerabilities to cause major damage in each of the six threat/vulnerability areas I previously enumerated, depending on their objectives.

Cyber Risk Formula

The Cyber risks concept brings everything together by relating threats and vulnerabilities in a formula. Risk can be described as the probability that a vulnerability will be exploited by a threat actor. It also considers the impact of that exploitation on a critical asset and is typically represented by a simple formula: risk = threat × vulnerability × impact. The impact is then a qualitative assessment of the impact level to the asset in question. For example, if the web application we are evaluating is for an e-commerce business such as Amazon, and an attacker is able to take down the website for a couple of hours, the impact level would be high for that particular vulnerability. Why? Because Amazon is primarily an e-commerce business that makes quite a bit of money per hour. Let us assume that Amazon makes $15 million per hour. If a particular vulnerability was exploited that resulted in two hours of downtime, this would cost Amazon approximately $30 million. This is called a high-impact vulnerability. Putting it all together, we come up with a risk score or rating based on these factors. Table 5 provides an overview of some potential scores for this fictitious web application example. It is important to note that risk scores can be subjective based on the subject matter expert's level of expertise or bias toward certain types of threats and vulnerabilities. So please keep in mind that most risk ratings are qualitative at best—unless a numerical rating scale is used (e.g. High = 7–10).

The process we just went through of identifying threats and vulnerabilities, and computing some rudimentary risk ratings, is called a cyber risk (or security/

Table 5 Cyber Risk Ratings

Cyber threat (table 2)	Cyber vulnerability (table 4)	Impact/risk	
Information will not be kept secret	Data exposure	Medium	Medium
Information cannot be trusted	Data manipulation	High	High
Information will not be available when it is needed	Denial of service	High	High
Identity cannot be verified	Identity spoofing	High	Medium
Access to resources cannot be verified	Unauthorized access	Medium	Low
The source of information received cannot be verified	Source identity spoofing	Low	Medium

threat) assessment. At a high level, a cybersecurity risk assessment identifies the various information assets that a cyberattack could affect (such as hardware, systems, laptops, customer data, and intellectual property), and then identifies the various risks that could affect those assets. As shown, it is a comprehensive way to look at how an attacker can exploit a target in a variety of ways. A cyber risk assessment can inform purchasing decisions for users or help companies prioritize cyber defense resource spending. Finally, let's consider the process by which this exploitation takes place. This is called the cyber kill chain model.

Cyber Kill Chain

The media, especially TV shows and movies, depict cyber-security attacks in a sexy and fast-paced way. The hacker is often a nerdy-looking character who is able to penetrate the most complex systems or networks in a matter of minutes or hours. This all occurs with various screens popping up, showing the apparent exploit they are executing against a target. One of my favorite movies of all time is *Swordfish*. In the film, a covert counterterrorist unit called Black Cell seeks money to help finance its war against international terrorism. Its leader, Gabriel Shear, brings in convicted hacker Stanley Jobson to help him. In one scene, Stanley must prove himself by hacking into a US Department of Defense system in sixty seconds. As the clock ticks, he tries a variety of different techniques. Later in the movie, he is asked to find and deploy a worm he created in college that steals money from a series of micro-transactions in major banks across the world. For this feat, he has a few days before his time is up again.

Although exciting to watch, movies and shows like this minimize the time, effort, and knowledge required to effectively penetrate even the simplest of networks, much less one that is as secure as the Department of Defense. For example, none of the steps Stanley uses are actually found in the kill chain model. As I explore the steps of a cyberattack and provide a real-world illustration, not a Hollywood one, it becomes clear why each step is required.

The cyber kill chain process, developed by Lockheed Martin, identifies seven steps that adversaries must complete in order to achieve their objective.[2] They are:

Step 1: Reconnaissance—The act of performing recon on a target to gain information about potential weak points that can be exploited (e.g., harvesting email addresses).

Step 2: Weaponization—The act of creating an exploit based on weaknesses identified in the previous step (e.g., if a company is using a vulnerable application or service, design an exploit for this service).

Step 3: Delivery—The act of delivering the exploit (often called a payload) to the target network or device (e.g., sending the exploit via email in the hope that an employee will download it).

Step 4: Exploitation—Once an exploit is successfully delivered, this step is the act of the application running on the victim machine to take advantage of the weakness identified in step 1 (e.g., a vulnerable version of Adobe Reader).

Step 5: Installation—This step goes along with step 4 in that once the exploit is successful, malicious code (the payload) will be installed on the victim machine.

Step 6: Command and control—Part of any exploit is the ability to correspond with the attacker from the victim machine. This step indicates that the payload will have a component that allows an adversary to do this (e.g., the communication channel between victim machine and "home").

Step 7: Actions on objectives—The act of executing the objective against a target. Usually, this action is data theft, but it may also be a denial-of-service or deception-based attack (e.g., phishing or social engineering).

Now let's look at a real example that shows the cyber kill chain in action. In 2013, Target was the subject of a cyberattack that resulted in the theft of approximately 110 million shoppers' financial and personal information. The US Senate's Committee on Commerce, Science, and Transportation did an outstanding job of putting together a report that aligns the kill chain with the actual breach.[3] I summarize its findings here:

Step 1: Reconnaissance—The attacker sent emails to a Target contractor, phishing for information, and performed internet searches to map the internal network structure.

Step 2: Weaponization—This step is not detectable by cyber defense techniques because it occurs off-line after the weakness is determined. In this step, the attacker prepared the exploit based on the information gathered in step 1.

Step 3: Delivery—The attacker delivered the payload in an email to the Target contractor through spear phishing (targeted email attack).

Step 4: Exploitation—Once delivered, the malicious application started to record credit card swipes and store data for later theft (step 7).

Step 5: Installation—As implied by step 4, the application had to be installed prior to being able to record the credit card transactions.

Step 6: Command and control—The attacker maintained a foothold on Target's network for over a month. Thus there is a reasonable assumption that there was a communication channel open between the victim's machine and the attacker (although this is unconfirmed in the report).

Step 7: Actions on objectives—The attacker transmitted the stolen data to outside server locations.

As you can see, there is quite a bit more involved in executing a cyberattack than is shown on a TV show or infomercial. The process of targeting and attacking a victim machine or network is complex as well as lengthy. For movie lovers, even the beloved *Hackers* of 1995 depicts hacking in a context that is somewhat unrealistic. In the film, hackers are blamed for creating a virus that will capsize five oil tankers. An attack of this magnitude would require all seven of the stages enumerated above, yet on film it is easier and more exciting to portray the actual attacks after the prework has been done. For example, one of the hackers is arrested and charged with crashing 1,507 computer systems in a single day and causing a single-day seven-point drop in the New York Stock Exchange. While the single day of the attack is conveyed, a number of unseen steps had to occur prior to this (e.g., identifying the systems, installing bot programs on the machines, and programming the crash time logic—when to execute). Because it isn't as thrilling to watch, the work that goes into planning an attack never makes it into the news and is left out of movie plots. In reality, though, that work is crucial to the successful execution of a cyberattack using the kill chain model.

MALWARE IN ACTION

You wake up in the morning in a great mood. Yesterday you found out you got a promotion and raise because of your outstanding performance with your company's clients. This is going to be a *great* day, and you try to get to work early. You speed through your regular morning routine and get to work an hour ahead of time. Sure enough, there is an email from the vice president of human resources with instructions on how to "claim your promotion." Without thinking about it, you click on the email and open the PDF attachment. Part of the instructions require you to download a new promotion tool kit that was specially designed to aid in the promotion process, so of course you follow the instructions exactly.

Around this time, your coworkers begin to arrive, and some walk by to shake your hand and offer you congratulations. This day could not get *any* better! The application finishes installing around the time your supervisor, Harry, gets in. You can hardly contain your excitement, so you let him know that you got in early to clear your schedule for any new tasks assigned to you given your new role. He's impressed by your initiative! Next you inform Harry that you received the email from human resources and already took care of installing the promotion tool kit, but you have some questions. The look on Harry's face is priceless as he asks the two-word question: "What email?" You repeat yourself and then realize that he wasn't joking.

You walk back to your computer with Harry to see a crowd of coworkers gathered around your desk. Every few seconds, frustrated screams rise from your colleagues that sit closest to you. Figure 6, shown below, is now on your screen, indicating that you have been hit with a ransomware attack and all your files are inaccessible.

Before long, the ransomware has infected the entire office. The day that started early also ended early—with you carrying a box to your car in shame.

So what was the meaning of all that? What happened, and how could it have been avoided? Malware is any software intentionally designed to cause damage to a computer, server, client, or computer network. In this unfortunate case, you were exposed to one of the most damaging and costly forms of malware—ransomware. Such attacks typically involve the infection of a single machine, which allows the attacker to hold data hostage on an organization's server or even a cloud-based server. All malware has its similarities, but they can be unique in their damaging effects. Let's learn some more about this dangerous cybersecurity issue.

Malware Overview

The primary goal of malware is to gain access to sensitive information or prevent the access of authorized users to this information. Malware comes in a variety of different forms, such as the Creeper virus and Morris worm discussed in chapter 1. In the rest of this chapter, I'll take a look at some of these forms along with some relevant examples.

As early as 2006, researchers were examining the most popular types of malware found in peer-to-peer (P2P) networks, which involve the sharing of resources between interconnected computer systems. At that time, peer-to-peer networks were a common means of sharing information online. As a result of the aforementioned convenience versus security challenge, little protection was put in place to make sure that the files exchanged in these networks were not malicious. Therefore this made peer-to-peer networks an ideal medium for spreading malware. This premise holds true today: malware is most prevalent in business sectors with a high volume of users and low security. In 2018, while the world was focused on Trojans (information stealers) and hackers mining for Bitcoin, the ransomware problem was quietly getting worse. Although this is not a book on cyber hygiene, this is a common theme with attackers. Wherever there are technology innovations, malware evolution is soon to follow.

Malware Class Background

There are two main classes of malware: host based and independent. As their names suggest, host-based malware requires a host in order to execute, and independent malware does not. The most common types of malware that require a host are viruses, Trojans, and logic bombs. The most common types of malware that do not require a host are zombies (aka bots) and worms. Further distinguishing the classes of malware, there are those that replicate and those that do not. Viruses, worms, and zombies form the classes of malware that replicate. Figure 6 depicts these malware classes.

A computer virus is code that replicates by inserting itself into other programs. A program that a virus has inserted itself into is infected and referred to as the virus's host. An important caveat is that viruses, in order to function, require their hosts; that is, a virus needs an

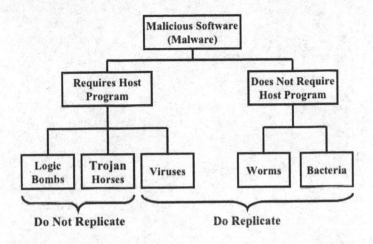

Figure 6 Malware class taxonomy.

existing host program in order to cause harm. For example, in order to get into a computer system, a virus may attach itself to some software utility (e.g., a word processing application). Launching the word processing application could then activate the virus that may, for instance, duplicate itself and disable malware detectors enabled on the computer system. A Trojan horse, or Trojan, is a type of malware that is often disguised as a legitimate application. Its goal is to gain system access by going in through the front door. A computer user is typically tricked into loading and executing Trojans. Once activated on a system, a Trojan can enable an attacker to spy on you, steal data, and open the back door to your system.

A virus needs an existing host program in order to cause harm.

A logic bomb, or slag code, is malicious code that is programmed to damage a network under certain conditions. The logic bomb metaphorically explodes when it is triggered by specific events, such as a certain date or time, the deletion of a specific file, or the launch of an infected application.

In contrast, worms do not need a host to cause damage. A computer worm replicates itself by executing its own code independent of any other program. Another distinction between viruses and worms is their propagation model. In general, viruses attempt to spread through programs/files on a single computer system. Worms, however, spread via network connections with the goal of infecting as many computer systems connected to the network as possible; recall the Morris worm example. Worms often hide within an OS that is either automated or otherwise invisible to the user. What gives them away is when their uncontrolled replication drains system resources, slowing or halting other tasks.

A zombie (also known as a bot) is a computer that has been taken over by a remote attacker who then sets it up to forward spam and viruses to other computers on the internet—either for sport or financial gain. Attackers typically exploit multiple computers to create a botnet, or zombie army. The increasing prevalence of home-based personal computers connecting to the web and remote servers via high-speed connections makes them more susceptible to such attacks.

The types of malware I've just reviewed form the basis for all other types of malware. Today, most malware is a combination of traditional malicious programs, frequently including parts of Trojans and worms, and occasionally a virus. Usually malware programs gain entry as Trojans, but once executed, they attack other networked systems like a worm. There are many other popular malware types, including spyware (spies on user activity), rootkits (hides malicious programs), backdoors (secures remote access to a computer system), and adware (generates unsolicited advertisements).

Although the modern world faces hacking by criminals or nation-states that could threaten everyone's way of life, the early days of malware were free of malice. Back then, the intention was to see what was truly possible with computing, not to harm, steal, or manipulate. Computing visionary John von Neumann was the first to have the idea for a virus, or a self-replicating string of code.[1] In 1949, he postulated the potential for a "self-reproducing automata" that would be able to pass along its programming to a new version of itself. This early research resulted in both the Creeper virus and Morris worm. In the next two sections, I am going to deconstruct viruses and worms into their logical components, and present a couple infamous examples to give you a better understanding of how they work.

Two Infamous Viruses: Melissa and ILOVEYOU

Viruses are primarily comprised of five distinct components: search routine, copy routine, infection mechanism, trigger mechanism, and the payload. Once a virus makes its way onto a computer system, the search routine looks for a host application to which it attaches itself. After the application has been identified, the copy routine is executed to merge the virus code into the target application. The infection mechanism is how the virus will spread and/or propagate throughout a system (or network, in the case of a worm). The trigger mechanism is the code that activates the virus. This could be an independent trigger mechanism (e.g., time bomb that executes at a certain date/time) or user-triggered event (e.g., a double click). All previous steps lead up to the execution of the payload, which represents the code that does the damage and achieves the virus's objectives. I will use this structure to describe the viruses in this section.

Melissa is a fast-spreading virus that is distributed as an email attachment that when opened, disables a number of safeguards in Word 97 or Word 2000, and if the user has the Microsoft Outlook email program, causes the virus to be resent to the first fifty people in each of the user's address books. While it does not destroy files or other resources, Melissa has the potential to disable corporate and other mail servers as the ripple of email distribution becomes a much larger wave. On Friday, March 26, 1999, Melissa caused the Microsoft Corporation to shut down incoming email. Intel and other companies also reported being affected.

The Computer Emergency Response Team, funded by the Department of Defense, issued a warning about the virus and developed a fix. The team responds to cyber incidents (or hack attempts) targeting Department of Defense information systems and networks. The technical analyses below are adapted from the Symantec, F-Secure, and University of California at Davis analyses of the viruses.

Search routine: When a user opens the infected document (LIST.doc), the search routine initiates a search for an email application (Microsoft Outlook) to connect to and sends up to fifty emails (for the potential infection of other users).

Copy routine: After sending itself out, the virus continues to infect (copy itself to) other Word documents and will attempt to replicate this process until it is eradicated.

Infection mechanism: When a user opens or closes an infected document, the virus first checks to see if it has sent this mass email once before. It does so by checking a registry entry. The registry or Windows registry is a database of information, settings, options, and other values for software and hardware installed on all versions of Microsoft Windows OS. If the entry has been found, this is an indication that the mass emailing (fifty emails) has already been done and it will not be done again. Otherwise, the mass emails will be sent.

Trigger mechanism: If the user downloads and opens an infected file (e.g., LIST.doc), the virus will execute. The virus will also execute independently based on the conditions described below.

Payload: As its primary payload, the virus will attempt to use Microsoft Outlook to email a copy of the infected document to up to fifty other people. There is a second payload that triggers once an hour, at the number of minutes past the hour corresponding to the date (i.e., on the sixteenth of the month, the payload triggers at sixteen minutes after every hour). If an infected document is opened or closed at the appropriate minute, this payload will insert the following sentence into the document: *"Twenty-two points, plus triple-word-score, plus fifty points for using all my letters. Game's over. I'm outta here."*

Another infamous virus arrives as a phishing email with an attachment (like a JPEG image file) with the subject line "ILOVEYOU"; when clicked on, the file in the ILOVEYOU virus sends the same email to everyone on the recipient's Microsoft Outlook contacts list. And it even deletes certain files on the recipient's hard drive. Thanks to Outlook's popularity among major corporations, on May 4, 2000, the virus spread so quickly that email had to be shut down by a number of major enterprises, including Ford Motor Company. The virus infected an estimated forty-five million users that day.

Here's a technical analysis of how the ILOVEYOU virus works:

Search routine: First, it executes a routine that locates each fixed and remote drive, and recursively goes through all their folders. In each folder, it looks for specific file types that it has been programmed to delete.

Copy routine: This is the main routine, which copies the worm into a root folder in the OS. The copy routine directs the injection of the virus into specific file types (as mentioned above).

Infection mechanism: This mechanism spreads the worm throughout all the victim's addresses in their address lists, similar to the Melissa virus. Alternatively, the virus can spread via Internet Relay Chat, a messenger service that was a precursor to applications like WhatsApp. The infection mechanism also uses the same method to determine if the mass mail message was already sent out (e.g., a registry entry).

Trigger mechanism: The user has to click on the file containing the virus in order for it to execute (e.g., a JPG or JPEG file).

Payload: On fixed and remote drives, Visual Basic, ActiveX, Java, and picture files are replaced by copies of the worm, so when the user double clicks on the icon corresponding to the file, the worm is launched. Movie files are simply hidden, but a worm file with the same name is created, giving a similar effect to the replacement of the other file types.

An Infamous Worm: Stuxnet

Worms share some of the same structural elements as viruses, but are typically made up of the following parts: target locator, infection propagator, remote control and update interface, life cycle manager, payload, and self-tracking mechanism. The target locator is similar to the search routine for a virus, although where a virus is looking for a host application to attach to, a worm is typically looking for propagation mechanisms such as email addresses or other target systems (identified via scanning for neighboring systems via IP addresses). The infection propagator is the mechanism used to transfer the worm onto another target system and infect the next machine. Next the worm creator uses the remote control and updated interface to communicate with the worm and provide updates. For example, if the target systems were Windows machines with Microsoft Office 2007 and these systems were updated to Microsoft Office 2010, the worm could communicate this, and the creator could update the worm code to target the new application type. The life cycle manager will run versions of the worm for a certain period of time and then update it based on preset conditions. All previous steps lead up to the execution of the payload, which represents the code that does the damage and achieves the worm's objectives. Optionally, worm authors might want to track the traversal path of the worm or keep track of victim machines. The self-tracking routine accomplishes this task. I will use this general structure to describe the Stuxnet worm in this section.

The Stuxnet (created by US and Israeli intelligence groups) worm targets so-called supervisory control and data acquisition systems, which are used widely for industrial control systems such as power, water, and sewage plants as well as in telecommunications and oil and gas refining. Stuxnet contained code that could identify software used in the logic controllers designed by German manufacturer Siemens. Logic controllers automate critical industrial processes such as temperature, pressure, and the flow rate of liquids and gases. Stuxnet was reportedly used to hijack high-speed centrifuges at Iran's uranium enrichment facilities, causing them to shake violently, which led to physical damage of the equipment.[2]

Here is an analysis of how this worm operates:

Target locator: Once on a machine, Stuxnet looked for Microsoft Windows machines and then sought out Siemens Step7 software, which is Windows software used to program industrial control systems that operate equipment (e.g., centrifuges).

Infection propagator: Stuxnet enters a system via a connected USB device and then executes the target locator routine (above). The worm would then propagate via printers connected to the internet exploiting a specific vulnerability.

Remote control and update interface: The worm was controlled remotely by two servers in Denmark via two IP addresses that were registered to false names, making them hard to track. Stuxnet was designed to spread on isolated networks, however, and therefore had been designed to be autonomous, reducing the need to have robust and fine-grained "command and control."

Life cycle manager: Different variants of Stuxnet targeted five Iranian organizations, with the probable target widely suspected to be the uranium enrichment infrastructure in Iran. This implies that the code had a means to swap out versions as necessary.

Payload: The worm forced the centrifuges to spin quickly for fifteen minutes and then return them to normal speed. Within five months of the attack, the excessive speed changes caused the machines to break, resulting in the loss of about a thousand centrifuges.

Self-tracking mechanism: There is no documented evidence of Stuxnet having a self-tracking mechanism built in. This is because it was required to be stealthy and operate on unconnected infrastructures. Yet the code itself had to be aware of newly compromised systems, which came online based on the communication mechanism built in (i.e., infecting neighboring machines).

MODERN-DAY APPLICATIONS

Would you be surprised to know that you use cybersecurity on a day-to-day basis? Given the ubiquitous presence of technology today, cybersecurity also permeates many aspects of our lives. Let's examine some statistics around technology and internet use. Close to 60 percent of the world's population uses the internet.[1] According to a 2019 Pew Research report, 81 percent of people in the United States say they go online daily, including 28 percent who are almost always online. Only 10 percent of adults say they do not use the internet at all. Among mobile internet users, 92 percent go online daily and 32 percent are almost always online. Roughly half of eighteen- to twenty-nine-year-olds say they are virtually always online, and 46 percent go online multiple times per day.[2]

Anytime a person uses some internet-connected technology, they are leveraging cybersecurity principles, whether intentionally or not. In this chapter, I will cover a number of common use cases such as authentication mechanisms, user identity, TLS, electronic commerce, banking, and blockchain technology. The goal of this chapter is to highlight how cybersecurity has proliferated our daily lives and societies.

Username and Password

The username and password paradigm dates back thousands of years in the physical world. Having to provide a secret code to gain access to a back room or tavern has been in existence for millennia, and is portrayed in countless modern movies and stories. The mindset behind applying username and password authentication is that end users would be the only people who know their passwords, and this would be enough to keep them secret and their accounts safe. But when hackers and attackers were able to discover end users' passwords without having to ask the user—by using brute force attacks and tools, such as the password cracker John the Ripper, with just dictionary words and simple combinations—the username and password paradigm had to shift.[3] Storing passwords with a random salt mask became common to keep passwords protected on the disk where they are stored. Forcing end users to change their password every thirty, sixty, and ninety days made attacking end users harder since their target to attack kept changing. Additional length and character requirements for passwords also made brute force attacks more difficult.

Yet even with all the safeguards, rules, and policies in place to make username and password combinations more secure, if MFA isn't used, as discussed in chapter 2, usernames and passwords are still susceptible to the aforementioned cyberattacks. MFA serves as a complement to password-based authentication by adding a factor (or factors) required for complete authentication. Recall how in chapter 2 I presented the fact that a fully secure authentication system would encompass the following:

- Something you know (username and password)

- Something you have (MFA token)

- Something you are (biometrics, as discussed in the next section)

A typical method of MFA would send an SMS message to your phone with a number combination that you have to enter after successfully entering your username and password combination. Not only does this add another authentication step, it requires an attacker to have physical access to the mobile device you have registered. This method may seem foolproof and completely secure, but what happens if you forgot that you loaned someone your old phone or it was stolen? Or worse yet, what if you upgraded to the latest Android or Apple device, and forgot to do a secure wipe before turning it in? The next time you attempt to authenticate to that particular web application, your pin will be sent to that device. This will reveal the site that you are authenticating to, deny you access to the site, or (in the case of a stolen phone) provide a potential entry point for an attacker into that application.

Biometrics

Biometrics offer extra layers of security when gaining access to accounts and include all metrics that are considered unique to every human. Biometric research is being conducted in areas such as fingerprint identification, ear structure, and retina scanners.[4] It is one of the ways to add heightened security by forcing end users to include both information about what you know (i.e., your username and password combination) and something you are (i.e., your fingerprint, EKG reading, or eye scan).[5] Biometrics is the missing link in a fully secure authentication system. It has become more common as image scanning is being used on various OSs (iOS and Microsoft) to unlock devices, and fingerprint scanning technology has become pervasive and is included on most modern laptops and smartphones. As image recognition technology continues to improve, facial and other physical features can be used to recognize and even authenticate people to gain access. Though there are many positive uses of biometrics, and in sci-fi movies (e.g., *Star Trek*) it can do intriguing actions like opening large metal doors to secret underground laboratories, image recognition gives rise to a number of privacy concerns. For example, fingerprints have been used for years to uniquely identify people. The issue with fingerprints, however, is that they are stored like passwords in databases. Storing fingerprints, facial images, and other biometric images in this way potentially exposes these databases to being breached since they are protected by some of the same mechanisms they store. Research and discussions around privacy concerns will continue as the use of these access control techniques increase in practice.

For now, the question arises, if biometrics are the strongest form of authentication, why not just use them and do away with other mechanisms? What could be stronger than a biometric-based authentication system? Hopefully by this stage of the book, you know that DiD is a principle that should always be employed in designing a secure system. Additionally, good security systems are both secure and usable by end users without disrupting the original intended use case of the item being secured. Fingerprint scanners are integrated into the device for ease of use. So, for instance, if every time you needed to use a fingerprint scanner on your mobile device you had to plug something in, you would probably stop using it after a while. Because biometric systems are sometimes not user friendly, they alone will not address all the issues with authentication. Lastly, the major challenge with biometrics is how to handle compromises. When a username or password is compromised or forgotten, it is easy to click the "forgot password" link and go through the process of resetting one or more of your credentials. I'm sure we've all done that many, many times! What happens if and when a biometric "credential" (fingers, toes, or eyeballs) is compromised? Similarly, in tactical environments such as the army, how do you leverage biometrics when soldiers are required to wear gloves with their standard-issue uniforms as well as some form of eyewear. These are some of the challenges that make the use of biometrics difficult for some modern-day cases.

VPNs

Internet access has become a public expectation rather than a commodity only for those with business needs or those willing to pay for mobile subscriptions. With more publicly available and easy-to-access internet sources, keeping communications and network transactions private and between expected end users has become more important than ever. Thus VPNs were created to keep end users' network traffic protected and private while still on a public network. This type of technology is akin to driving on a busy highway with millions and millions of other cars, but you are able to drive safely in your own lane. Your personal lane connects you as an end user to any destination where you would like to go. This lane also exists for as long as you are on the road as well as when you arrive at your destination and are done driving. At that point the lane is repurposed for someone else to use. VPNs are used to keep private network communication private while still providing access to the internet.

A VPN works by routing your device's internet connection through a chosen private server rather than your internet service provider. It acts as an intermediary and conceals your IP address. If your data is somehow intercepted, it will be unreadable until it reaches its final destination. This process is illustrated in figure 7.[6]

The primary challenge with using a VPN is the infrastructure required. As you may have guessed, VPN tunnels share some similarities with SSL/TLS, which form the basis for secure (HTTPS) connections. HTTPS secures information communicated between a person's web browser and a website. It is indicated in green in the browser address bar and also by a padlock icon. While this does indeed provide added security while web browsing, your data will still be vulnerable, particularly if you're using public Wi-Fi. If

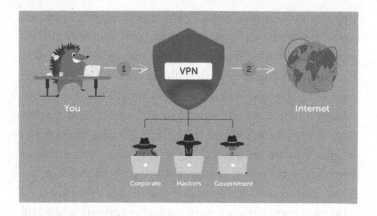

Figure 7 VPN example.

anonymity online is worth it to you, then VPNs add an effective layer of security and are one of the more common forms of cybersecurity used online today.

E-commerce

Modern society is an online one. Communication, experiences, and even shopping can all be done online, so much so that traditional brick-and-mortar storefronts are closing due to a lack of foot traffic and business. Many people would rather shop online, and with Amazon's Prime delivery, you wait only one to two days before the item is delivered to your front door—the ultimate convenience factor. That said, with this convenience comes quite a range of cybersecurity concerns, most of which are centered around data protection and user privacy. This was never more apparent than in 2014 when the e-commerce site eBay was breached, and reportedly 145 million users' account information was potentially viewed and exfiltrated.[7] Such a breach would be cause for concern even for the most secure organizations, but eBay is unique since, supposedly, its account information was stored in plaintext. This means there was no encryption to mask the actual username, email address, phone number, physical address, and date of birth of its users. This may seem innocuous and innocent, but this type of information can be used to launch attacks on other platforms. Think of the common questions that are asked by password reset protocols on platforms such as email. Usually they will ask for answers to one or more of the personally identifiable metrics that were jeopardized in the eBay breach. This could lead to catastrophic breaches, hacks, and unauthorized access across multiple sites, perhaps even on banking websites.

This breach was also interesting because of how the attackers gained access. Reportedly the hackers used three employee log-in credentials to gain access to the large database of user accounts. This suggests that social engineering attacks such as phishing or vulnerable browsers were exploited to retrieve these unsuspecting employee accounts. Applying cybersecurity to e-commerce represents a challenging problem as it must protect data for both end users and the employees who have access to the end user data. How would you protect end user accounts? How would you change the level of access for employees? These are difficult questions that have a snowball effect on how systems are implemented and how businesses operate online. Modern e-commerce systems such as Amazon have advanced to the point where their use is secure. Thus as a general user, it is important to use reputable vendors when shopping online.

Banking, Tokens, Payment Systems, and Brokerage Systems

Virtual tokens are another way that authorization can be provided when a user needs to frequently access a secured system. Tokens rely on various cryptographic algorithms. Soft(ware) tokens, for instance, are locally stored apps that allow for two-factor authentication beyond just a username and password. They are loosely based on the Kerberos cryptographic algorithm, which was designed at MIT to provide strong authentication for client and server applications by using secret key cryptography. A good example is Apple Pay and other smart device payment systems, which utilize soft tokens authorized by the various payment companies that represent physical credit and debit cards owned by the end user. This algorithm basically uses a central server to grant soft authentication tokens to various devices. These soft tokens provide the ability for these devices to act as an authenticated user, granting the device any access control capabilities that the end user approves. Consumers can use these soft tokens to purchase goods just as their physical credit cards would work in stores.

Soft tokens are great for gaining easy access to systems without having the physical token—that is, credit card. This type of access also requires stringent control over how and what devices are authorized to gain access via soft tokens. MFA can be used to ensure the correct device is authorized to access systems via soft tokens. Soft tokens also provide the ability to decouple username and password tokens from system access. In this case, if an attacker were to view an account being accessed, without possession of a soft token, they would not be able to associate the log-in credentials with the soft token to log in. This effectively creates an authorization process that is anonymized, as the soft token is associated with specific log-in credentials but cannot be used to identify a particular user.

Blockchain Technology

An online society provides great flexibility and access to information—more access than was ever imagined. With great access, though, comes a greater need for accounting. Keeping track of all the various communications, transactions, and activities online seems like a nearly impossible task. But one technology that has been used to record the activities and transactions happening online is blockchain. Better known for its application to Bitcoin and other cryptocurrencies, blockchain at its core is technology that records data using cryptographic algorithms, ensuring that the actions and activities that are recorded cannot be denied. This process of nonrepudiation guarantees that an action executed by Person A was in fact executed by Person A and cannot be denied in the future. Blockchain technology also removes the need to have a single controlling party (like a private corporation or central bank) review and capture every record of online activity. This process (called decentralization) allows for more efficient recording and provides higher integrity than traditional methods since blockchain technology is based on cryptography.

In terms of cybersecurity, this could alter how end users interact with the internet as third-party hosting fees could effectively disappear, and all transactions would occur directly between supplier and consumer. This could also make transactions more efficient and secure since they could be publicly verified and proven. Some of the more common use cases for blockchain technology are as follows:

Banking and finance: Cryptocurrencies serve as a unifying currency that can be ubiquitously used across the world without a third-party arbitrator.

Digital identity: Identity credentials could be stored on blockchain to preserve immutability and make auditing easier whenever the credentials are used within a registered system.

Government: Government regulations require annual compliance audits across a number of domains. Blockchain could be used as an immutable repository for enforcing regulatory compliance as well as auditing various compliance standards.

Health care: Data control and exchange based on blockchain can make medical data management, including drug and medical device tracking, more efficient.

Law: Blockchain introduced the concept of a smart contract, which is a digital representation of an actual legal document.

Publishing: Blockchain can serve as a viable replacement for digital rights management of such content as music or e-books. The copyright rules and requirements could be stored and enforced via blockchain technology.

Supply chain management: Blockchain can facilitate the accurate and transparent tracking of products and services from manufacturing all the way up to the point of consumption.

Smart Devices

Smart devices have changed the face of technology potentially more than any device in history. They provide their owners with a computer in their hands that they can access at any time, connecting more people than ever before. With this increase in connectivity comes the need to improve security around networking, user recognition, and protecting personal information. Smartphones have advanced to incorporate many of the core tenants of cybersecurity. Confidentiality is used to encrypt photos, texts, and other data on the device. Integrity is used to ensure apps are doing what they should do and have not changed without the device owner's knowledge. Accessing the device itself incorporates both what you know and who you are to include pin and biometric log-in capabilities. Nevertheless, because of all the information that is stored on these devices, including health information, personal text messages, and pictures, there is a need to heighten their security. Hackers are interested in controlling and accessing information on smart devices. Phones, tablets, smart watches, and other devices have to incorporate form factor technology to be thin, lightweight, and efficient as well as secure, locked down, and controllable, all while being usable. Many times, these three concepts are difficult to integrate, but smart devices have been able to integrate them on a consumer-friendly device that is here to stay.

IoT (Internet of Things)

IoT is a fancy term for smart devices that can connect to the internet, including baby monitors, vehicles, medical devices, network routers, and consumer electronics.[8] There may be as many as twenty billion IoT devices in use today. Unsurprisingly, such devices are attractive to hackers. For example, Mirai is malware that infects smart devices that run on ARC processors, turning them into a network of remotely controlled bots or zombies. Mirai scans the internet for IoT devices that run on this particular type of processor, which runs a stripped-down version of the Linux OS. If the device's default username and password combination is not changed, Mirai is able to log into the device and infect it. This is just one of the instances of attacks that target IoT devices.

With this in mind, there is a treasure trove of data that an adversary can harvest from an IoT device. Such devices are particularly susceptible to attacks against the six cyber tenets I presented in chapter 1. The security protections, however, have not necessarily caught up to the capabilities. In some cases, IoT devices (e.g., automatic lights, video doorbells, and baby cameras) add security as an orthogonal effect. By this I mean that both provide protection when you are away from your home (or the baby's room) and give the appearance that you are "always home."

CYBERSECURITY FOR THE FUTURE

In this final chapter, I will discuss a number of innovative cybersecurity research areas that are worth noting: outcome-based cyber defense, artificial intelligence / machine learning, and Computer immunology. Outcome-based cyber defense focuses on attack outcomes rather than the attacks themselves. Recall that there are three primary cyberattack outcomes: denial-of-service attacks, data theft attacks, and misinformation attacks (i.e., cyber deception). Denial-of-service attacks prevent legitimate users from accessing systems or data that belong to them. Data theft attacks remove information that pertains to authorized users. Misinformation attacks cause legitimate users to make decisions based on erroneous information (e.g., phishing).

In recent years, as data volumes have increased, artificial intelligence is being applied in various areas of cybersecurity in an attempt to emulate the function of a human

Outcome-based cyber defense will use the detection system as a trigger only.

being in decision making.[1] Machine learning is a subset of artificial intelligence that has both supervised and unsupervised methods of analyzing information that is useful for cybersecurity. A supervised approach will take labeled data and learn from it for subsequent examples, while an unsupervised approach will learn from unlabeled data. Natural immune systems protect animals from dangerous foreign pathogens, including bacteria, viruses, parasites, and toxins. Their role in the body is analogous to that of computer security systems in computing. Although there are many differences between living organisms and computer systems, the similarities are compelling and could point the way to improved computer security.

Computer Immunology

The analogy of computer immunology with human immunology contributes an important point of view about how to achieve computer security—one that can potentially lead to systems built with entirely different sets of assumptions, biases, and organizing principles than in the past. Immunologists have traditionally described the problem solved by the immune system as that of distinguishing "self" from dangerous "other" (or "nonself"), and eliminating the dangerous nonself. The issue of protecting computer systems from malicious intrusions can similarly be seen as the problem of distinguishing self from nonself, which might be an unauthorized user, foreign code in the form of a computer virus or worm, unanticipated code in the form of a Trojan horse, or corrupted data. What would it take to build a computer immune system with some or all of the properties of a natural immune system—especially one that is outcome focused? Advances in multicore computing systems, networking, mobile and smart devices, sophisticated software, and the internet have enabled the development of revolutionary capabilities that have served many fields across industry, the military, and academia. But these advances have also led to vulnerabilities resulting from the complexity of the various platforms and their respective applications. Current security techniques are mainly labor intensive (e.g., patch update), signature based, and not flexible enough to handle the complexity of modern-day attacks. This is partly because cybersecurity approaches are often based on attack prevention.

The field of autonomic computing, which investigates principles of self-management and self-healing, serves as a viable baseline for exploring immune system principles in today's computing environment. We require an autonomous decision-making system that can adapt, react, and learn from real-time computer systems to keep up with the pace of cyberattacks, which requires a complementary paradigm shift from focusing on attack prevention to attack outcomes or effects. Such a system would have much more sophisticated notions of identity and protection than those afforded by current OSs, and would provide a general-purpose protection system to augment current computer security systems. It would have at least the following components: a stable definition of self, prevention or detection and subsequent elimination of dangerous foreign activities (infections), a memory of previous infections, a method of recognizing new infections, and a method of protecting the immune system itself from attack. Immunological models are experimental systems that re-create aspects of the human immune system to study its development and function in health as well as disease. In the computing world, the major challenge will be to replicate elements of the immune system that are applicable in the computing space. To mitigate this risk, existing immunological models can be mapped onto relevant computing functions—specifically at the OS layer. OS security is the process of ensuring OS integrity, confidentiality, and availability. OS security refers to specified steps or measures used to protect the OS from threats, viruses, worms, malware, or remote hacker intrusions.

Outcome-Based Cyber Defense

While computer immunology centers on the proactive prevention of cyberattacks, outcome-based cybersecurity assumes an attack will inevitably occur, and concentrates on preventing the outcomes or objectives of an attack. A simple example of outcome-based cyber defense for denial-of-service attacks would be a system designed with built-in redundancies. Denial-of-service attacks are often caused by overwhelming the capacity of a server. The traditional cyber defense would focus on detecting an attack and starting to drop traffic that would overwhelm the server to prevent further damage. Outcome-based cyber defense will use the detection system as a trigger only. The trigger will instruct the backup system to take over if the primary system goes down. Outcome-based cyber defense can also be used for malware detection. Current antimalware products are designed to look for signatures (or indicators) of malware being downloaded or installed on a computer system. If the signature matches a file or a pre-specified behavior of an executable file, it will be blocked or quarantined for further analysis to ensure that it does not infect other files. The outcome-based alternative to this approach would be to categorize malware based on the specific outcome it is trying to achieve. Based on that outcome and the system objective, it will either allow or deny the malware from running. For example, if the system objective is to serve as a payroll processor and the malware is designed to change non–payment file extension names, then that malware can be allowed to run. This approach is distinct from and more efficient than the signature-based method described above. By design, it will consume fewer resources because it will only be polling for malware that can negatively affect a system's objective.

A similar approach can be employed for data theft or a misinformation attack. With data theft, the outcome we are trying to prevent is the unauthorized removal of data leaving a network or machine. This is called extrusion detection. For this to be effective, sensitive data needs to be tagged and examined whenever an attempt is made to transfer it from the system or network. If the attempt is made by an authorized user, allow it. Otherwise the attempt should be denied. Misinformation attacks can be prevented similarly. In the case of a misinformation attack, what is the outcome we are trying to prevent? Deception. So users have to be able to trust their information systems and data within these environments. I discussed many integrity mechanisms in chapters 2 and 3. A combination of system integrity, data integrity, and digital signatures (for data transmitted over a network) can suffice to offer legitimate users confidence in the systems they use, data with which they interact, and information they receive. We still have a long way to go before we get ahead of the adversary completely. To close the gap, we need more research that focuses on defense methods based on outcomes.

Artificial Intelligence / Machine Learning

One of the aspects of artificial intelligence that is most applicable to cybersecurity is machine learning. Machine learning uses statistical techniques to give computers the ability to learn (i.e., progressively improve performance on a specific task) with data, without being explicitly programmed. Imagine you are the administrator of a network with a hundred thousand machines that could potentially be hacked. It would be impossible for you to monitor all the machines to determine if they were behaving strangely. Machine learning allows you to form a baseline of the "behavior" of a user and an associated computer system. Then it can identify any aberrations from this behavioral norm and generate an alert. Now you only have to look for new behaviors that might be indicative of an attack.

A good supervised machine learning example would be identifying how long it would take you to walk around the neighborhood. You could feed the algorithm information such as age, physical condition, weather information, distance, and details from previous similar walks. The data would be labeled accordingly, and the estimate determined by the "supervised" algorithm. Alternatively, an unsupervised example that is commonly used is the identification of an animal (e.g., a dog) based on its unique characteristics. If someone interacts with a dog and begins to notice that it has fur, long floppy ears, a distinct smell, walks on all fours, a specific body shape, and barks—these are "features" or characteristics that could be used to identify another dog. No one has to supervise the identification and characterization of these features; they will be recognized automatically through repeated interactions with previous dogs.

Anomaly detection is the process of spotting unusual activity, data, or processes (e.g., fraud detection for online banking or gambling). Anomaly detection principles are different from traditional intrusion detection in that they do not require a signature to detect aberrant behavior or traffic of concern. Once the machine learning algorithm (supervised or unsupervised) has established the baseline of normalcy within an environment, the anomaly detection engine can begin to detect anomalies. Research in this area has focused primarily on attack detection, as is the trend with most cyber products and conceptual ideas. When considering an outcome-based approach to anomaly detection, how could we employ these techniques to *prevent* the attack outcomes of deception, data theft, or denial of service?

For instance, mobile apps exist that aim to improve the user experience when checking voice mails. They can filter incoming calls and transcribe incoming messages to text. They can even detect fake (deceptive) calls, which show up as phone numbers that seem familiar. These apps can play an out-of-service message and hang up the phone (preventing the scammer from leaving a voice message). This is an excellent case of why it is essential to focus on attack outcomes. These voice mail apps are also an example of natural language processing, which enables computers to understand the ways humans speak through the analysis of natural language data. The government intelligence community uses this technique heavily to intercept chatter that could identify homeland security threats. Conversational artificial intelligence and natural language processing platforms can help companies automate routine communications tasks like customer service, internal help desks, knowledge management, and member engagement. Amazon's Alexa is a good example of a natural language processing technology that is able to produce results with little voice input. These technologies use statistical machine learning methods to extract conversational intents and entities from natural language input. For cybersecurity, this capability would be most helpful in the pursuit of an advanced persistent threat, which involves an unauthorized user gaining access to a system or network, and remaining there for an extended period without being detected. The artificial intelligence engine could preserve this "context" (once initially detected either via anomaly detection or a signature-based system) and initiate recovery measures when the attack resumes.

Take the example of an attack that is planned over a few days:

Day 1: we will socially engineer using the help desk

Day 2: we will plant a logic (time) bomb on victim machines

Day 3: we will release the virus at 8:00 p.m. on Sunday

To fully understand the attack, all the messages need to be collectively combined to form a "case" against an adversary. A mechanism for preserving context makes this possible.

Conclusion

What is the cybersecurity of the future? Put it this way: it is about simultaneously keeping one eye on new technology innovations and one eye on cybersecurity's foundational past, all with a perspective that is more focused on preventing attack outcomes than the attacks themselves. Researchers have noted that social media users tend to overshare life details that can be used maliciously by cybercriminals to access sensitive accounts and steal the user's identity. This frightening observation underscores the need for cyber hygiene and for users to be aware of their part in advancing the "state of the art" in the cyber defense community. Remember, the first step of the cyber kill chain is reconnaissance, where an attacker selects a target system or network, performs research, and looks for vulnerabilities. Part of this research is called open-source intelligence gathering, which is data that criminals can collect from publicly available sources. The quality of open-source intelligence is directly proportional to data available to the public. Oversharing life details on social media provides open-source intelligence data, which can subsequently be used in the remaining steps of the cyber kill chain, specifically weaponization.

I encourage you to take from this book whatever principles resonated with you most. I hope that through reading this book and others on the topic, you will gain an appreciation for a field that is still in its infancy but is rapidly evolving day by day. When in doubt, recall the cybersecurity tenets as you encounter new topics that will undoubtedly emerge, even during your further reading about this subject. Foundationally, cybersecurity is as simple as the preservation of these tenets:

1. Confidentiality: keeping information secret

2. Integrity: maintaining information correctly and reliably

3. Availability: ensuring information is available to the right people at the right time

4. Authentication: verifying an identity

5. Authorization: verifying access to resources

6. Nonrepudiation: validating the source of information

GLOSSARY

Access control list
List specifying the access permissions for a file

Actions on objectives
The last step of the cyber kill chain indicating the intention of an adversary against a target (e.g., denial of service or information theft)

Application Security
A cybersecurity approach aimed at protecting the confidentiality, integrity, and availability of an application

Artificial intelligence
Imitation of intelligence by machines

Authentication
The process of identifying and verifying a user

Authorization
Providing users with appropriate permissions to access information

Availability
Ensuring that data is consistently accessible by the intended users

Biometrics
Physical or behavioral human characteristics that can be used as a form of authentication

Blockchain
A digital record (blocks) of transactions across multiple computers that are not controlled or distributed by any one entity

Bot
A computer that is infected with malware and is under the control of an attacker

Cipher
Algorithm used to perform encryption or decryption

Cloud computing
On-demand availability of computer system resources via the internet and an associated web service for various purposes, including storing data (larger quantities) or processing data (faster or more efficiently)

Cloud/mobile security
A cybersecurity approach aimed at protecting the confidentiality, integrity, and availability of mobile devices along with the data they store in cloud environments

Command and control
The communication channel through which a malicious application (e.g., malware) installed on a victim machine communicates with its creator (e.g., hacker application or actual person)

Compliance
Meeting a regulatory requirement for some aspect of cybersecurity protection (e.g., personally identifiable information safety)

Computer immunology
A cybersecurity approach that is modeled after the human immune system

Computer security
A cybersecurity approach aimed at protecting the confidentiality, integrity, and availability of a computer system

Confidentiality
Ensuring that information is kept undisclosed

Creeper virus
Arguably the first computer virus; displayed the words I'M THE CREEPER: CATCH ME IF YOU CAN" on infected printers

Cryptographic algorithm
A set of mathematical instructions used to encrypt or decrypt data

Cryptography
The original form of cybersecurity focused on protecting the confidentiality and integrity of data through encryption and hashing algorithms

Cybercrime
A criminal activity that involves the use of a digital asset to conduct the crime

Cyber hygiene
A measurement of how safe a user is online based on their online habits

Cyber kill chain
The steps an attacker takes to successfully exploit a target

Cybersecurity
The availability, integrity, authentication, confidentiality, and nonrepudiation of electronic communications

Data security
A cybersecurity approach aimed at protecting the confidentiality, integrity, and availability of data

Defense in depth (DiD)
Layered approach to cyber defense; if one layer fails, the attack can be prevented at another layer

Digital signature
A digital representation of a human signature enabled through cryptography

Encryption
Two-way cryptographic function for providing data confidentiality through the use of symmetric or asymmetric keys

E-voting
Casting ballots via electronically

File permission
Provides read, write, and execution privileges for a file

Firewall
A cyber defense tool that blocks or denies network traffic based on predefined rules

Hacking
The "art" of attacking a target computer system, network, or person

Hashing
One-way cryptographic function for providing data integrity

Hypertext Transfer Protocol Secure (HTTPS)
A secure connection to a website that uses the Secure Sockets Layer to maintain the confidentiality of data transferred between a browser and web server

ILOVEYOU virus
A worm that targeted Windows' computers with a malicious file attached to an email title "ILOVEYOU"; also known as the love bug and love letter

Integrity
Ensuring that data remains untainted or uncorrupted

Internet of Things (IoT)
A term used to describe anything (a device or machine) that is connected to the internet

Kerberos
A network protocol that utilizes tickets to provide authentication and communication over a network

Logic Bomb
Code that is hidden in a system that does not act until certain conditions are met

MAC
A unique computer/device identification number

Machine learning
A science that utilizes algorithms to develop computers that can simulate intelligence without being programmed

Malware
Software that is designed to do harm to a computer system (e.g., a mobile device or personal computer)

Melissa virus
A virus that infected Microsoft applications, causing multiple emails to be sent overloading systems

Misinformation attack
An attack that causes users to make decisions based on false information

Morris worm
A self-replicating computer program that was designed to see how large the internet was, but ended up causing more harm than good

Multifactor authentication
A form of authentication that requires two or more credentials to verify the identity of a person for access

Network security
A cybersecurity approach aimed at protecting the confidentiality, integrity, and availability of a network

Nimda
A worm that would attach itself to files sent via email (first released in September 2001)

Nonrepudiation
Principle guaranteeing that information such as a message or transaction cannot be deemed invalid

Open Systems Interconnection (OSI)
A conceptual model that describes the way in which computer systems communicate through layers

Open Web Application Security Project (OWASP)
Consortium that publishes information about web application vulnerabilities and mitigation activities

Outcome-based cyber defense
A form of cyber defense that focuses on preventing the intended outcome (i.e., information theft) of a cyberattack rather than preventing the attack itself

Password
A secret word or phrase that must be used to gain admission to something

People security
A cybersecurity approach aimed at protecting the human layer of security (e.g., social engineering or phishing)

Phishing
A targeted social engineering attack that attempts to get a user to click on a link that will download malware or input credentials on a fake website

Public key infrastructure (PKI)
Technology that provides certificates for people and devices to authenticate themselves online; the certificates can also be used to supply integrity, nonrepudiation, and confidentiality

Ransomware
A type of malicious software (malware) that takes over a computer or system in order for an attacker to demand money for access

Risk
The possibility of a system being exposed to a cyberattack

Secure Sockets Layer (SSL)
A layer 6 (Open Systems Interconnection model) protocol for securing a connection between a client and server

Secure software development life cycle
A method for integrating security into each phase of the original software development life cycle

Social engineering
The act of using a social connection (i.e., trust relationship) to get a user to perform an action leading to an attack

Stuxnet
A worm, identified in 2010, that is designed for supervisory control and data acquisition systems

Threat
An entity that can exploit a vulnerability

Transport Layer Security (TLS)
An updated version of the Secure Sockets Layer protocol that is more secure and efficient

Trojan
A type of malicious software (malware) that infects a system by hiding in legitimate software or applications

Virtual private network (VPN)
A service that provides a secure connection to a network via the internet

Virtual token
An exterior device that is used to provide access to a system other than the use of a password

Virus
A type of malicious software (malware) that utilizes a host computer or system to self-replicate

Vulnerability
A characteristic of a computer system that puts it at risk of being attacked

Weaponization
The act of creating an attack for a specific target

Worm
A form of a computer virus that can replicate itself and infect multiple computers in a network

NOTES

Chapter 1

1. "History of the Enigma," Crypto Museum, accessed June 4, 2019, https://www.cryptomuseum.com/crypto/enigma.

2. "Creeper Virus," Techopedia, August 18, 2011, accessed August 8, 2020, https://www.techopedia.com/definition/24180/creeper-virus.

3. Margaret Rouse, "Elk Cloner," WhatIs.com, September 21, 2005, accessed August 8, 2020, https://searchsecurity.techtarget.com/definition/Elk-Cloner.

Chapter 2

1. "Measuring Digital Development: Facts and Figures 2019," ITU, accessed August 11, 2020, https://www.itu.int/en/ITU-D/Statistics/Documents/facts/FactsFigures2019.pdf.

2. Tim Berners-Lee, "Tim Berners-Lee's Proposal," "CERN, May 1990, accessed August 11, 2020, http://info.cern.ch/Proposal.html.

3. Patrick Nohe, "How to Fix the SSL/TLS Handshake Failed Error," SSL Store, November 14, 2018, accessed August 11, 2020, https://www.thesslstore.com/blog/tls-handshake-failed.

4. Archana Prashanth Joshi, Meng Han, and Yan Wang, "A Survey on Security and Privacy Issues of Blockchain Technology," *Mathematical Foundations of Computing* 1, no. 2 (2018): 121–147.

5. Shanhong Liu, "Blockchain—Statistics and Facts," Statista, March 13, 2020, accessed August 11, 2020, https://www.statista.com/topics/5122/blockchain.

6. Jack Stromberg, "Uptime Percentage Chart," n.d., accessed August 13, 2020, https://jackstromberg.com/uptime-percentage-chart.

7. Amarendra Babu L, "Cloud Computing Trends in 2019," January 7, 2019, accessed August 13, 2020, https://hub.packtpub.com/cloud-computing-trends-in-2019.

8. Thomas J. Law, "19 Powerful Ecommerce Statistics That Will Guide Your Strategy in 2020," December 2, 2019, accessed August 13, 2020, https://www.oberlo.com/blog/ecommerce-statistics.

9. "Advanced Field Artillery Tactical Data System (AFATDS)," Raytheon Techologies, n.d., accessed August 13, 2020, https://www.raytheon.com/capabilities/products/afatds.

10. John Spacey, "5 Examples of Non-Repudiation," December 20, 2016, accessed August 13, 2020, https://simplicable.com/new/non-repudiation.

Chapter 3

1. "Simple Substitution Cipher," Practical Cryptography, n.d., accessed August 13, 2020, http://practicalcryptography.com/ciphers/simple-substitution-cipher.

2. Shaan Ray, "Cryptographic Hashing," November 3, 2017, accessed August 13, 2020, https://hackernoon.com/cryptographic-hashing-c25da23609c3.

Chapter 4

1. "The Ultimate List of Cyber Security Statistics for 2019," PurpleSec, n.d., accessed August 14, 2020, https://purplesec.us/resources/cyber-security-statistics.

2. Max Kanat-Alexander, "The Purpose of Technology," Code Simplicity, February 14, 2014, accessed August 14, 2020, https://www.codesimplicity.com/post/the-purpose-of-technology.

3. Mellissa Withers, "Social Media Platforms Help Promote Human Trafficking," November 22, 2019, accessed August 14, 2020, https://www.psychologytoday.com/us/blog/modern-day-slavery/201911/social-media-platforms-help-promote-human-trafficking.

4. Peter G. Neumann, "Security Criteria for Electronic Voting" (paper presented at the Sixteenth National Computer Security Conference, Baltimore, September 20–23, 1993), accessed August 14, 2020, http://www.csl.sri.com/users/neumann/ncs93.html.

Chapter 5

1. Leo Kershteyn, "Cyber Threat Basics, Types of Threats, Intelligence and Best Practices," SecureWorks, May 12, 2017, accessed August 14, 2020, https://www.secureworks.com/blog/cyber-threat-basics.

2. "Proactively Detect Persistent Threats," Lockheed Martin, n.d., accessed November 25, 2019, https://www.lockheedmartin.com/en-us/capabilities/cyber/cyber-kill-chain.html.

3. US Senate, Committee on Commerce, Science, and Transportation, "A 'Kill Chain' Analysis of the 2013 Target Data Breach," March 26, 2014, accessed August 14, 2020, https://www.commerce.senate.gov/services/files/24d3c229-4f2f-405d-b8db-a3a67f183883.

Chapter 6

1. "When Did the Term 'Computer Virus' Arise?," *Scientific American*, October 19, 2001, accessed August 14, 2020, https://www.scientificamerican.com/article/when-did-the-term-compute.

2. Kim Zetter, "An Unprecedented Look at Stuxnet, the World's First Digital Weapon," *WIRED*, November 3, 2014, accessed August 14, 2020, https://www.wired.com/2014/11/countdown-to-zero-day-stuxnet.

Chapter 7

1. "Internet Growth Statistics," Internet World Stats, n.d., accessed August 15, 2020, https://www.internetworldstats.com/emarketing.htm.

2. Andrew Perrin and Madhu Kumar, "About Three-in-Ten U.S. Adults Say They Are 'Almost Constantly' Online," Pew Research Center, July 25, 2019, accessed August 15, 2020, https://www.pewresearch.org/fact-tank/2019/07/25/americans-going-online-almost-constantly.

3. Jeff Petters, "How to Use John the Ripper: Tips and Tutorials," Varonis, March 29, 2020, accessed August 15, 2020, https://www.varonis.com/blog/john-the-ripper.

4. Simon Liu and Mark Silverman, "A Practical Guide to Biometric Security Technology," *IT Pro* (January–February 2001): 27–32.

5. "Three-Factor Authentication: Something You Know, Something You Have, Something You Are," Thales, September 5, 2011, accessed August 15, 2020, https://dis-blog.thalesgroup.com/security/2011/09/05/three-factor-authentication-something-you-know-something-you-have-something-you-are.

6. "How Does VPN Work?," Namecheap, n.d., accessed August 15, 2020, https://www.namecheap.com/vpn/how-does-vpn-virtual-private-network-work.

7. Jeffrey Roman, "eBay Breach: 145 Million Users Notified," Information Security Media Group, May 21, 2014, accessed August 15, 2020, https://www.bankinfosecurity.com/ebay-a-6858.

8. Samuel Greengard, *The Internet of Things* (Cambridge, MA: MIT Press, 2015).

Chapter 8

1. "The Big Data Facts Update 2020," NodeGraph, n.d., accessed August 15, 2020, https://www.nodegraph.se/big-data-facts.

FURTHER READING

Bejtlich, Richard. *The Tao of Network Security Monitoring: Beyond Intrusion Detection*. Boston: Addison-Wesley Professional, 2004.

Bejtlich, Richard. *Extrusion Detection: Security Monitoring for Internal Intrusions*. Boston Addison-Wesley Professional, 2005.

Cappelli, Dawn, Andrew Moore, and Randall Trzeciak. *The CERT Guide to Insider Threats: How to Prevent, Detect, and Respond to Information Technology Crimes (Theft, Sabotage, Fraud)*. Upper Saddle River, NJ: Pearson Education, 2012.

Clarke, Richard A., and Robert K. Knake. *Cyber War: The Next Threat to National Security and What to Do about It*. New York: HarperCollins, 2010.

Erickson, Jon. *Hacking: The Art of Exploitation*. 2nd ed. San Francisco: No Starch Press, 2008.

Graham, James, Richard Howard, and Ryan Olson, eds. *Cyber Security Essentials*. Boca Raton, FL: Auerbach Publications, 2011.

Hadnagy, Chris. *Social Engineering:The Art of Human Hacking*. Indianapolis: Wiley, 2018.

Howard, Michael, David LeBlanc, and John Viega. *19 Deadly Sins of Software Security: Programming Flaws and How to Fix Them*. 1st ed. New York: McGraw-Hill, 2005.

Hubbard, Douglas W., and Richard Seiersen. *How to Measure Anything in Cybersecurity Risk*. New York: John Wiley and Sons, 2016.

Johnson, Thomas A., ed. *Cybersecurity: Protecting Critical Infrastructures from Cyber Attack and Cyber Warfare*. Boca Raton, FL: CRC Press, 2015.

McClure, Stuart, Joel Scambray, and George Kurtz. *Hacking Exposed: Network Security Secrets and Solutions*. New York: McGraw-Hill, 2003.

Meeuwisse, Raef. *Cybersecurity for Beginners*. Raleigh, NC: Lulu, 2015.

Mitnick, Kevin D., and William L. Simon. *The Art of Deception: Controlling the Human Element of Security*. New York: John Wiley Sons, 2003.

Mitnick, Kevin D., with Robert Vamosi. *The Art of Invisibility: The World's Most Famous Hacker Teaches You How to Be Safe in the Age of Big Brother and Big Data.* 1st ed. New York: Little, Brown and Company, 2017.

Schneier, Bruce. *Applied Cryptography: Protocols, Algorithms, and Source Code in C.* 2nd ed. New York: John Wiley and Sons, 1995.

Schneier, Bruce. *Data and Goliath: The Hidden Battles to Capture Your Data and Control Your World.* 1st ed. W. W. Norton and Company, 2015.

Shoemaker, Dan, and Wm. Arthur Conklin. *Cybersecurity: The Essential Body of Knowledge.* Boston: Cengage Learning, 2011.

Sikorski, Michael, and Andrew Honig. 2012. Practical Malware Analysis: The Hands-On Guide to Dissecting Malicious Software *Practical Malware Analysis: The Hands-on Guide to Dissecting Malicious Software.* 1st ed. San Francisco: No Starch Press, 2012.

Stoll, Cliff. *The Cuckoo's Egg: Tracking a Spy through the Maze of Computer Espionage.* New York: Doubleday, 1989.

Zetter, Kim. *Countdown to Zero Day: Stuxnet and the Launch of the World's First Digital Weapon.* New York: Broadway Books, 2015.

The MIT Press Essential Knowledge Series

DUANE WILSON is an avid learner and loves to mentor others who are new to the field of cybersecurity. He has a number of advanced degrees but is most focused on spending time with his family, playing basketball, practicing piano, and ministering to others.